BULLY-PROOFING CHILDREN

A Practical, Hands-On Guide to Stop Bullying

JOANNE SCAGLIONE
ARRICA ROSE SCAGLIONE

Rowman & Littlefield Education
Lanham, Maryland • Toronto • Oxford
2006

Published in the United States of America
by Rowman & Littlefield Education
A Division of Rowman & Littlefield Publishers, Inc.
A wholly owned subsidiary of The Rowman & Littlefield Publishing Group, Inc.
4501 Forbes Boulevard, Suite 200, Lanham, Maryland 20706
www.rowmaneducation.com

Estover Road
Plymouth PL6 7PY
United Kingdom

British Library Cataloguing in Publication Information Available

Library of Congress Cataloging-in-Publication Data

Scaglione, Joanne, 1946–
  Bully-proofing children : a practical, hands-on guide to stop bullying / Joanne Scaglione, Arrica Rose Scaglione.
        p. cm.
  Includes bibliographical references.
  ISBN-13: 978-1-57886-507-9 (hardcover : alk. paper)
  ISBN-10: 1-57886-507-7 (hardcover : alk. paper)
  ISBN-13: 978-1-57886-508-6 (pbk. : alk. paper)
  ISBN-10: 1-57886-508-5 (pbk. : alk. paper)
 1. Bullying. I. Scaglione, Arrica Rose, 1978–   II. Title.
  BF637.B85S368 2006
  302.3–dc22

                                                          2006015372

∞™ The paper used in this publication meets the minimum requirements of American National Standard for Information Sciences—Permanence of Paper for Printed Library Materials, ANSI/NISO Z39.48-1992.
Manufactured in the United States of America.

To POPS,
For your patience, love, and unending support
for all that we do.

Put yourself in the shoes of a victim of bullying. Everyday a child is bullied is an eternity to them. We worry about terrorists coming into our country and doing harm to us. A victim of bullying walks into their school each day knowing their terrorist could strike any moment and destroy their wounded spirit again and again. How long can a child "play on the freeway dodging cars" before the experience finally becomes too much and they go over the edge?

Brenda High
Executive Director, Bully Police USA

CONTENTS

INTRODUCTION   xi

PART 1   AN OVERVIEW **Understanding
the Problem**   1

1   **WHAT IS BULLYING?** A Snapshot   3

2   **CYBERBULLYING** Technology Ushers
in a New Brand
of Bullying   7

3   **WHY BULLYING?** A Dilemma   15

4   **HOW COMMON IS IT?** The Real Hard
Facts and Statistics   20

5   **IF UNCHECKED** The Consequences   23

6   **WHAT CAN WE DO TO ARM
OUR CHILDREN?**   28

PART 2   THE PROFILES **Who Are the Players?**   31

7   **IDENTIFYING THE BULLY**   33

8   **WHO ARE THE VICTIMS?**   36

CONTENTS

9 THE BYSTANDER Support for the Bully   40

10 CLIQUES VERSUS FRIENDS   45

PART 3 HOW TO SPOT BULLYING
        The Red Flags   49

11 WHAT ARE THE SIGNS?   51

12 ASK THE RIGHT QUESTIONS
    Kids Will Answer   55

PART 4 WHAT CAN YOU DO?
        Antibully Solutions   61

13 OPEN THE COMMUNICATION GATES   63

14 LITERATURE AND REAL-LIFE
    STORIES HELP CHILDREN LEARN
    AND UNDERSTAND   69

15 DEALING WITH THE BULLY   116

16 TAKING AWAY SUPPORT FOR
    THE BULLY An Effective School Program   124

17 COPING STRATEGIES FOR VICTIMS   128

18 CLASSROOM-TESTED LESSONS
    Work in the Home and in School   142

PART 5 A PROACTIVE APPROACH
        FOR PREVENTION   173

19 CREATE A BULLY-PROOF
    ENVIRONMENT   175

20 TEACHING CONFLICT RESOLUTION
    A Valuable Tool   188

21 TEACHING FRIENDSHIP SKILLS
    Making and Keeping Friends   200

CONTENTS

APPENDIX Recommended Children's Reading List   213

REFERENCES   217

ABOUT THE AUTHORS   219

INTRODUCTION

Bullying seems to be approaching epidemic proportions in our schools today. On campuses we've seen bullying reach heightened levels resulting in serious school violence. The killings at Columbine High School in Littleton, Colorado, on April 20, 1999, were a reminder that bullying is not a fact of life. When two teenagers were bullied and tormented so cruelly by others, they resorted to murder for revenge.

As a parent, teacher, counselor, and administrator for more than 30 years, I have witnessed the growing problem of bullying on elementary, middle, and high school campuses. My daughter and coauthor has watched it escalate over the past 20 years firsthand as a student. As early as five years of age, "blossoming" bullies can be observed in kindergarten classrooms. It seems to hit a peak during the junior high school years.

Unfortunately, for too long it has been denied, ignored, and, sad to say, accepted as "part of life." Meanness, put-downs, and other forms of harassment and abuse toward individuals seem to be admired qualities that are glamorized in our society. Just turn on your television set. Popular shows like *Jerry Springer*, *Survivor*, *American Idol*, and *Apprentice* thrive on put-downs, rejection, and cruel insults like "You're fired," "You're out," and "You're terrible." These are the wrong messages to send kids if we want to raise children to respect each other and care about each other's feelings.

In order to stop bullying, we need to begin with our children. Our children are our future. They represent the next generation of citizens, who in turn will be the role models for the next generation, and so on. All children need to understand that bullying behaviors are wrong. They need to embrace the Golden Rule and learn how to get along with each other. They need to learn empathy (and yes, it can be learned) and how to appropriately deal with all feelings, including anger. Conflicts need to be accepted as part of life, and kids need to be taught how to peacefully resolve them. Zero tolerance for bullying everywhere and anywhere should be the mantra. Lastly, children need to learn how not to be victims and to support each other. In short, we need to begin the bully-proofing process early on to break the chain. The only remaining questions for us are where, when, and how to do this.

Raising children to be kind begins in the home and should continue in schools. Parents must set good examples for their children. It's the old adage: "The apple doesn't fall too far from the tree." Children learn early on how to behave in part by watching their parents. They are like sponges. They will imitate and copy parents' behaviors, whether we want them to or not. Remember, more often than not they do as we do and not as we say if our actions contradict our words. At home, parents need to understand that in fact they are their children's first and primary teachers until the children go to school. From ages birth through five, when children enter kindergarten, the parents will build that foundation from which future behaviors will spring. Being loving, caring, and accepting is how parents must start. What parents model and teach children during these years is crucial to their development. A parent's job includes creating opportunities for children to interact with other children, monitoring and guiding their behaviors, building empathy, and teaching them problem solving and conflict resolution. This is the time when parents can also teach children how *not* to be victims. Raising a confident child with strong self-esteem, a child who can stand up for himself or herself, is the best weapon to combat bullying. Teaching children strategies that will protect them from the bully is the child's best armor. Remember, just as a strong house requires a strong foundation, so too it is for the child.

The schools also have an important responsibility as well to bully-proof our children. A climate and program must be developed so that bullying cannot flourish nor survive on any school campus. When children enter school, a part of the curriculum should focus on character education, reinforce social skills and/or strengthen them where necessary, and validate positive qualities when they are demonstrated. Giving children opportunities to work and play together, setting clear rules and expectations, and delivering important life lessons on getting along should be a major part of the program. An antibullying curriculum must be taught in every classroom whereby all children learn to deal with bullies and support victims.

To this end, the authors have developed a comprehensive program whose mission is to bully-proof children. The acronym ECOS is the title for a program that had its roots in classrooms. Designed and tested as an antibully program in grades K–6, it has recently been expanded and revised using elements of many model school programs. It involves a coordinated four-part approach to raising children at home and in our schools. In short it stands for:

Educate all children on how to get along with each other and be kind
Confront bullies by setting limits on their behaviors and adopting **0** tolerance for bullying
Support victims by taking them seriously and teaching them bully-proofing skills

The essence of the program calls for both schools and parents to partner together to solve the problem of bullying. Each prong of this four-part approach must be implemented because each prong alone is insufficient to effectively deal with this issue. Only when parents and schools work together to deliver this antibully program will we effectively stop bullying.

This book is intended to educate students, parents, and teachers, so that there is a thorough understanding of how to deal with bullying, how to intervene to stop it, and how to be proactive to prevent it. Part 1 is intended to raise the level of awareness of the reader by giving an overview of the bullying problem. This part presents the what, where, why, and how of bullying. The increasing frequency of it and the resulting consequences demonstrate how seriously this issue must be taken. Parts 2 and 3 continue to explain the nuances of this phenomenon by describing the players and participants and how to spot signs of bullying. In part 4 antibully solutions are offered to mobilize entire schools and parents by working together to develop effective programs and policies. Detailed classroom-tested lessons on how to get along and erase bullying are presented for teachers and parents. Lastly, part 5 addresses proactively the prevention of bullying. Described here are the safe, healthy, and respectful home and school environments necessary so bullying cannot flourish. Moreover, lesson plans and strategies are presented for parents and teachers to teach important life skills such as anger management, problem solving, conflict resolution, and friendship.

May you use these tools to create environments where all children are safe and free from humiliation and have the right to learn so they may always find the strength to challenge any misfortunes that confront them in life. Raising healthy, resilient, and independent children now is the best gift we can give to the generations to come.

PART 1

AN OVERVIEW
Understanding the Problem

Before we can solve a problem, we need to face it and understand it. Arming our children against bullying requires that we have in our arsenal the answers to basic questions:

- What constitutes bullying?
- What is a cyberbully? How does he or she operate?
- Why do kids bully and become victims?
- How widespread is this problem?
- What are the consequences if we don't address it?

1

WHAT IS BULLYING?

A Snapshot

Peter hated walking to recess through the school hallways because others were always intentionally pushing and shoving him.

Jessica called Ashley "Fatso" ever since kindergarten.

Jason constantly received e-mails from classmates who called him a "nerd."

Nicole was the source of rumors all summer long. Danielle and others said she was "slut" and put it on the Internet.

Mallory told the others not to play with Jennifer. Jennifer always felt "left out."

The label "bullying" describes all of these behaviors. Bullying is aggressive behavior that includes a wide range of conduct and, as you can see, takes on a variety of shapes and forms. It can impact another's body, property, self-esteem, or social position. It can be physical, verbal, or emotional. It can involve teasing, name-calling, pushing, hitting, or even the more subtle behaviors that include intentionally ignoring or excluding someone or spreading nasty rumors.

A CONTROVERSY: DOES THIS DEFINITION WORK?

Our classic stereotypic snapshot of bullying—a "big brute" picking on a smaller or younger child, is indeed no more. Several new definitions have been put forth to describe the phenomenon; however, in practice they are not always effectively used. In fact, the definition of bullying has become somewhat controversial. Very different attitudes literally polarize opposing opinions as to what bullying is. The good news is that more and more people are seeing it more seriously today than ever before as an issue that needs investigation. However, how we define bullying takes on a great significance because our definition of the problem will lead us to the solution.

Theoretically (and please note the use of the word *theoretically*), the classic definition of bullying comes to us from Dan Olweus, considered the father of the bully movement. He has been doing research and intervention in the area of bullying for over 30 years. His antibully program was recently named as one of the top model programs used in American schools. He defines bullying as "aggressive behavior that (a) is intended to cause distress or harm, (b) exists in a relationship in which there is an imbalance of power or strength, and (c) is repeated over time" (Limber and Small 2003, 445).

According to this popular definition, three elements must be present in order to classify behavior as bullying:

1. There must be intent by the bully to cause another harm.
2. There must be an imbalance of power or strength between the bully and victim.
3. The behavior must be repeated over time.

However, our real-world observations seem to point out flaws in this definition. There are certain behaviors that don't include all three of the elements yet they are examples of bullying. An imbalance of power or strength would exclude often-seen acts where someone torments another of equal strength. Here is a good example: A beautiful girl newly enrolls at the school. The boys start paying attention to her. The popular clique of girls resent it and start a name-calling and rumor campaign targeting her as their victim. Our James Brenton story (see chapter 9) is another example. Accusing him of being a "rat," his friends turn on him. He is ostracized, and the group's sole goal is to make his life miserable. Day in and day out they torment him.

Moreover, the element of intentional harm may not always be present. Many bullies will tell you that they don't intend to hurt anyone but rather they are just having some fun. The reaction from the victim makes it a game, encouraging them to continue. This may explain why they don't target kids who laugh or ignore it . . . no fun. In fact, much research seems to indicate that the only things that bullies hope to get from their behavior are respect, power, and popularity from others.

A REALISTIC DEFINITION—THAT KEEPS CHANGING

Since the devastating killings at Columbine High School, schools have been developing strong antibullying programs and policies to prevent a reoccurrence. But because schools want so badly to create safe and peaceful environments for children, they seem to have broadened the definition of bullying. Today, in many instances, the term has become an umbrella for all aggressive behaviors by children. An aggressive child who easily "blows up" at others and has difficulty getting along with peers may be labeled a bully, when in reality his issue may be anger management. Depending on the nature of the bullying and motivation behind it, examined in chapter 3, there are two very different types of bullies. This may explain why a more expansive approach to defining bullying must be taken.

So then, how *do* we define bullying? In our opinion, it is aggressive behavior toward another, repeated over time, and it is deliberate and hurtful. It may or may not involve an imbalance of power or strength or an intention to harm another, depending on the motivation behind it. This definition requires three different elements to be present for us to label a behavior bullying. The behavior must be:

1. repeated over time,
2. a deliberate act, and
3. hurtful to another

BULLIES: A SNAPSHOT

A snapshot of bullying reveals that either an individual or a group can carry out bullying. In fact, many bullies have an entourage that is always present to support them. Both males and females engage in bullying behaviors. More recent studies seem to indicate that there are more male than female bullies. However, bullying patterns seem to be very different between boys and girls. Boys are more likely to bully in a physical manner. They will hit, push, kick, or slap. Girls, on the other hand, are more likely to verbally or psychologically bully their victims. Their brand of bullying is clearly harder to detect. Girls are more likely to spread rumors and gossip about their victims. They will purposely exclude others and try to keep others from being their friends. Ages vary from children to adults. The bully can be the same age or older or even younger than the victim. However, here our concern is with children. Unfortunately, we see the beginning of bully behaviors occurring in preschool- and elementary-age children. I as an elementary counselor for three years was surprised to find out how prevalent it was in grades K–5. Yet most studies seem to highlight the middle school years, grades 6–8, where it most frequently occurs.

2

CYBERBULLYING

Technology Ushers in a
New Brand of Bullying

With the miraculous wonders of the Internet and all that it has allowed us to do comes a downside or dark side that is hurting children. The schoolyard is being replaced in many cases by cyberspace as the place to harass others. And because one may now communicate anonymously through modern technology and never face a victim, bullies are becoming more vicious than ever. Advances in technology in the last 10 years have brought forth a new form of bullying, known as "cyberbullying."

Using information and communication technologies to bully others is the same as every other kind of bullying: an attempt to get control, power, and revenge over and from others. Only the tools used are different. Using e-mail, cell phones, and text messages in this way, along with instant messaging and defamatory websites, is a growing problem not only in the United States but also around the world. As more and more children use the Internet (almost all children are given access to it at a minimum in school) bullies are finding a new place, outside of school, to harass others. It has definite advantages for the bully. Anonymous and hard to track, it is safer for the bully. Because it is out of the jurisdiction of the school, the school may not pursue this type of bullying with disciplinary measures. And yet these technologies can spread gossip and rumors to thousands with a few strokes on the computer keyboard.

Cyberbullying behaviors are intended to hurt, frighten, and embarrass peers, just like every other kind of bullying. It may include posting on websites lies, attacks, photos, and gossip about their victims; sending ugly or threatening e-mails or instant messages; or using cell phones to send hundreds of e-mails to drive up a victim's cell phone bill. In many instances, ironically, previous victims of bullies are taking the opportunity to use the Web as a weapon to retaliate. The victims have found a way to get revenge by acting like bullies themselves. Students formerly labeled and attacked as "nerds" are getting even as cyberbullies skillfully attacking their predators. The bully/victim finally has a tool to confront the bully with anonymously.

CYBERBULLYING ON THE RISE

Cyberbullying has reached such proportions that "legislators, law enforcement officials, educators and members of Wiredkids Inc. met in Washington to discuss ways to help kids and parents handle internet bullying," according to Marianne Kolbasik McGee (2005).

Recently introduced in the House of Representatives, the Anti-Bullying Act of 2005 (H.R.284) requires states, districts, and schools to address the issue of bullying. They are to develop programs and policies to prevent and respond to bullying and harassment, including cyberbullying on schools' computers and other forms of technology. The bill further allows schools to apply for federal grants to develop and implement programs that would educate students and teachers about bullying.

A 2004 survey of 1,500 students in grades 4–8, conducted by i-Safe America (a nonprofit internet safety organization), revealed some worrisome statistics about the prevalence of cyberbullying:

42% of students have been bullied while online—25% more than once.

35% of students have been threatened online—nearly 20% more than once.

21% of students received mean or threatening messages through e-mail or other means.

58% of students report that mean or hurtful things have been said to them online—40% more than once.

53% of students have said mean or hurtful things to another online—one-third more than once.

58% of students have not told an adult or parent about mean or hurtful things said to them online.

SIGNS TO LOOK FOR

Adults need to be on the lookout for signs that cyberbullying may be occurring. Both parents and teachers need to watch carefully, because the consequences can be so devastating. Red flags, indicating it's time to ask questions, should go up when children:

spend a lot of time on the computer

seem particularly secretive or evasive about Internet activities

close windows on their computers as soon as an adult enters the room

claim they are doing long hours of homework

seem to spend long hours in chat rooms or at questionable websites such as schoolscandals.com

have unexplained pictures on the computer

have a long list of cell phone charges from the same phone number on the bill

CONSEQUENCES

The consequences of cyberbullying for the victim can be even more devastating and painful than other forms of bullying because of how quickly rumors and gossip can be spread over the Internet and the huge numbers of people these hurtful messages can reach. Being the target of a constant attack of lies and rumors spread by peers, especially on the Internet, is about the worst thing that could happen to a child. Anxiety, depression, shame, destruction of self-confidence and self-esteem, school phobia, and failing grades are a few of the potential by-products.

WHAT TO DO

Arming children against cyberbullies is a difficult task. Even the most involved and diligent parents are having a hard time not only understanding the technologies but also tracking the responsible parties. Children's use of things like instant messaging and text messaging available through AOL and MSN is something that many parents do not comprehend. However, the same advice on arming children against any bully applies here as well. Treat any incident of cyberbullying as you would any form of bullying (see part 4). The key is to keep the communication gates open. Encourage children not to keep this to themselves. Encourage the victims to find someone they can trust (hopefully it's the parent) to talk to about it. Reassure the victims that it is not their fault; more likely than not, they did nothing to deserve it.

Parents need to educate children as to how not to become a victim. Advise children to be very cautious as to whom they give an e-mail address or cell phone number to. This information is not available to the cyberbully unless the victim or a friend of the victim supplies it. In fact, tell children never to give out personal information or passwords. Passwords are secrets. Personal information includes your name, address, pictures of yourself, and so forth. Chat rooms are often the most dangerous places where kids inadvertently give this information to strangers. Children should be instructed not to open e-mails, messages, or attachments from anyone they don't know.

The next bit of advice may be a little difficult for children to digest. Explain to them that correct etiquette online, known as "netiquette," means being polite and kind to others. The Golden Rule applies to online behavior: Treat others as you would like to be treated.

Unfortunately, many of us treat others the way we are treated and make matters worse. Children need to learn to never send messages to others when they are angry. Advising children to "fight back" and match the cyberbully's rude behavior sends the wrong message to children and simply doesn't work.

Children should be advised not to respond to cyberbullies in any way no matter how tempting it is, no matter how much they want to, and they will want to. Remember this is exactly what the bullies want: some sort of reaction from the victims. They want to know that you are worried, scared, or upset. This is their reward. It gives them control and that feeling of power over their prey. Children should not answer or engage the bullies in any way through instant messaging, text messaging, or cell phone calls. They should not post a response to a derogatory message on a defamatory website like schoolscandals.com. If possible, they should block e-mails and instant messages coming from this sender. Many internet service providers (ISPs) do give consumers the ability to do this. If the cyberbully is online . . . close out and go off-line. If bullying does get severe, change your e-mail address or your cell phone number and give them out only to close, trusted friends. Without a target to attack, the cyberbullies may look elsewhere where the rewards are greater, where they can push someone else's buttons . . . where they can get a reaction.

If a child has become a serious victim of a cyberbully, a parent should notify their ISP or cell phone company and local police. Unfortunately, ISPs are often very reluctant to respond and the response time is very slow. Depending on the nature of the bullying, these agencies may be able to help discover the identity of the bully and/or take action to stop him or her. Where there is a defaming website involved, there have been cases where the website has been taken down after a threat of legal action. There is software to protect or discover the identity of who is sending harassing messages. Currently on the market are such programs as *Email Tracker Pro*, *McAfee Parental Controls*, and *Security Soft's Predator Guard* designed to track e-mails, offer chat filtering protection, and scan for threatening and harassing text. We however do not endorse any of these products since we have no knowledge of how reliable and effective they are.

IN THE SCHOOLS

Teachers and schools need to take a proactive approach to fighting every kind of bullying. Rules for cyberbully behavior (and all other forms of bullying) must be communicated to students and parents and followed through with consequences when broken. When bullies know they can get away with this behavior, they are much more likely to engage in it. Parents shouldn't be afraid to ask about the school's antibullying policy: What are the school rules, how are they communicated to kids, and how are they enforced?

Schools and classrooms should place all computers with Internet access in open, commonly used areas where there is foot traffic nearby. Remember that bullies do their bullying in a secretive manner so as not to get caught. Every school where computer use by students is the norm should adopt a contract that all students with access to a computer must sign and agree to follow before they are permitted to use a school computer. Certain behaviors must be prohibited and carry consequences if engaged in by a student, including at a minimum discontinued use of the school computer. Those activities pertaining to bullying should be listed specifically in the contract:

No harassing, insulting, or attacking others
No sending or displaying any information or pictures in any format that could be viewed as offensive
No sending unwanted e-mails or messages that are hurtful to another
No using another person's password or accessing another's folders, work, or files

Unfortunately, because bullies' number one priority is *not* to get caught, most cyberbullying generally occurs off campus and after school hours on children's home computers and cell phones. Schools have a difficult time serving up any kind of disciplinary action for this behavior because it is out of their jurisdiction. Once children are off school grounds and not on the way to and from school, the school has no power to control their acts.

WHAT CAN PARENTS DO AT HOME?

Parents should begin by becoming "cybersmart" so that they understand all aspects of the problem and can respond effectively. A May 2005 survey on parental Internet monitoring, commissioned by the National Center for Missing and Exploited Children (NCMEC) and Cox Communications reveals some scary statistics:

> 51% of parents do not have or know about monitoring software that tracks where kids go and whom they interact with.
> 42% of parents said they do not look at what their teens read or type in chat rooms or via instant messaging.
> 30% of parents reported that they allow their teenagers to use computers in private areas of their house, including their bedrooms. (Walsh 2005)

Parents can start by learning the Internet basics: from Internet language the kids use, to blog sites they visit, to tips on how to keep children safe online. Two of the largest online safety, education, and help groups, www.wiredsafety.org and www.isafe.org, can empower parents to face this issue head-on.

Parents need to take responsibility for their children's behavior online. Too often they are giving their children carte blanche to do whatever they like with no supervision of their activities online. For some children, it is like putting a weapon in their hands and hoping they are doing the right thing with it. Parents who do this need to be held accountable when their children use the Internet to bully others. The location of the computer in the home becomes significant. Many experts insist that allowing young people the privacy of a computer in their bedrooms is an open door for trouble. Without any supervision children can use the computer to satisfy any whim. The best place for the family computer is where there is a lot of family foot traffic. The family room does not give any privacy to engage in unacceptable behavior.

As for cyber behavior, everyone using the computer should be aware of what is and what is not acceptable. Children in the home should be responsible for their Internet behavior. At a minimum, clear rules as to Internet use must be established and all online activities must be monitored. Before a child is allowed access, a parent should put forth a contract (just like schools) as to what is acceptable. It should be quite clear that no teasing, bullying, or using the computer or cell phone (if it has Internet access) to hurt others would be tolerated. The rules should reflect that parents will be monitoring regularly children's Internet activities, and that if there is something that the children don't want the parents to see, then they shouldn't be engaging in it in the first place. Let them know that software will be loaded on the computer that will track their behavior.

3

WHY BULLYING?

A Dilemma

Understanding the "why" of bullying is the key that unlocks the door to solutions. Discovering the motivation behind bullying should be step one. Knowing and understanding the reasons helps us to support the victim and stop the bullying.

In most situations, the victims keep bullying a secret. They bury it deep inside themselves, usually blaming themselves in part or in whole for being victims. They let it continue, as it "eats away at them" and makes them feel worse and worse about themselves. They do not seek help because they are ashamed, embarrassed, or fearful. The victims need to understand why they are targets of bullies so that they can act to effectively put an end to it when possible. Similarly, the bullies need to get a handle on why they are engaging in this behavior and its effects on others.

BULLYING IS ABOUT POWER

Much of the recent research seems to indicate that, contrary to popular belief, most bullies do not suffer from low self-esteem. Feeling bad about themselves does not explain why they bully. In fact, they are usually well liked by their peers and by adults. They bully not to intentionally harm another but rather to obtain things that we all want in life: power, popularity, and respect from others.

Bullying in most respects is about power. In many societies money, talent, and fame are the ultimate ways to achieve power. We admire those who have power. In fact, within every society or social group, humans seek status and respect as they climb the ladder of success. The instinct to dominate is the desire for power and control. In schools, bullying is one way (though a negative one) children achieve respect and status from their peers. Bullies use their victims to feel powerful.

TWO TYPES OF BULLIES

Motivations for bullying vary, depending on the type of bully. Researchers generally distinguish between two types of bullies. "Pure" bullies are children that just bully, while combination "bully/victims" are children who bully others but are also victims of bullying themselves.

A "pure" bullying incident occurs generally when a victim is picked on for no apparent cause other than maybe appearance, size, or some trait that suggests vulnerability. Here the bully is looking for power and control over another and is out to have fun by teasing someone. Upon examining the pure bully and victim relationship, the uneven balance of power becomes evident.

The motivation of the pure bullies is usually power and domination. These bullies will pick on others they perceive to be weaker than themselves. They are rewarded when their victims react. Their behavior is reinforced when they make others feel sad or angry. They have little empathy for their victims. The reaction of the victims generally encourages the bully to continue to taunt them. This powerful feeling of being able to "push buttons" keeps the bullies returning for more.

On the other hand, the combination bully/victims selectively target their victims. Here the bully is operating with a "victim mentality." A victim mentality occurs when the bully thinks like a victim and acts from a base of anger and revenge. In effect, the victims respond to a situation aggressively because they are angry with someone. They feel like a victim but act like a bully. The perfect example of this bully/victim behavior was the violence at Columbine High School. Here the victims, harassed by others, became the ultimate bullies themselves. Research confirms that children who have been bullied by others often do become bullies themselves. In fact more and more children are becoming part of the increasing statistic of kids who bully and are bullied themselves. According to a study done by the National Institute of Child Health and Human Development (NICHD 2001), 6% of the children surveyed admitted to both bullying and being bullied.

OTHER FACTORS MAY PLAY A PART

We all get angry with others from time to time and feel victimized, maybe some of us more than others. But why is it that some children, when they get angry, aggressively attack others with words and actions? A number of factors may play a role in explaining why some children resort to bullying and others don't. Such factors as family dynamics; a previous history of being bullied; jealousy; or a desire to belong, or for attention, may help explain it.

The home situation may place children at risk for becoming bullies. All children need loving and nurturing homes in order to grow up into healthy, loving, and compassionate adults. When parents act as bullies in the home, their children often imitate their behavior. Negative and mean parents who regularly attack or put down their children produce offspring who will do the same to others. Often where warmth and demonstrative love is not part of the landscape, and where parents have a very minimal involvement with their children, the risk becomes greater. Where there is a lack of supervision by parents or other adults, the risk goes up. But keep in mind this does not imply that where two parents work long hours, there is a likelihood of them raising bullies. But couple the lack of warmth with lack of supervision and involvement and the risk does jump. Quality loving time and daily connecting with children on an emotional and caring level certainly offsets the risk of children becoming bullies in a household of two working parents.

The parenting style may also have something to do with raising children with aggressive and bully tendencies. The two extreme approaches of being too permissive or too strict may produce a similar result for different reasons. A permissive style, where parents do not set adequate limits for children's behavior, can produce out-of-control children. They tend to control their parents and everyone else in their lives. They have not learned self-control. These children do not expect to follow a set of rules but rather, set the rules themselves. They do what they want, when they want. Tantrums usually result when these children are unhappy with a parent request. On the other hand, the dictator or bully-type parents, who are overly tough and physical in disciplining, may raise children that rebel and/or learn to imitate them. These children learn to interact with others in a dominating and controlling manner. There is a necessary balance when it comes to setting limits and guiding children's behavior that is required (described in detail in part 5) in order to raise healthy and kind kids.

Some children may live in homes where they have been bullied by siblings. Where siblings have developed such a relationship, the risk increases. Siblings can be very cruel to each other. It's that old pecking order: The oldest picks on the middle child, who in turn picks on the youngest. However, where it is a daily occurrence for one brother or sister to tease and taunt another or just be plain mean or aggressive toward the other, with little cooperative play offsetting it and no effective intervention, the risk grows. This pattern of behavior engaged in for a long period of time may become ingrained in the children's personalities. Children who establish a pattern of bullying a younger sibling may bring this behavior to school. Similarly, that younger sibling who has been bullied may look for and find opportunities in turn to bully smaller children or continue to be a victim of others. It therefore behooves parents to be vigilant in raising their children. It is important to observe children's interactions with others, set and enforce clear rules in the home, and reward kind behavior toward siblings and others.

In discussions, children point to many reasons in addition to power, control, and revenge to explain why someone may come after them and mercilessly bully them. Jealousy, attention, and the desire to belong are the most common.

Jealousy can be a powerful motivating force for some children. There may be a desire by some to attack or just put down others who are perceived as "better" than they. For girls especially, jealousy can trigger mean-spirited behavior toward each other. A new girl comes into school and receives attention from the boys. She's beautiful. She may very well become a target. The boy that Alison likes is hanging out with Breanna. Breanna knows that Alison likes him but disregards it. Alison is so angry that she starts a bully campaign with Breanna as the target.

Bullies often get a lot of attention when they openly bully others. They feel like the "king of the mountain" and they believe others look up to them for it. Attention from others is attractive for a number of students. It is part of the desire for power, control, respect, and popularity that the pure bully craves.

Belonging is an incentive for some children to cross the line and bully others. Peer pressure can have negative effects. If a group of students makes fun of Jake, others may follow suit to feel they are like the others; they belong. Being part of a clique sometimes requires its members to support and participate in bully activities of the group.

4

HOW COMMON IS IT?

The Real Hard Facts and Statistics

"[Bullying is] a public health problem that merits attention."
—Duane Alexander, M.D., director of the NICHD

A variety of recent studies involving different age groups point to some alarming statistics. The findings from these studies are staggering, considering that so many incidents of bullying have gone unreported until now, with victims often remaining silent due to fear of reprisals, embarrassment, or shame.

Bullying is widespread in American schools, says a study by the National Institute of Child Health and Human Development (NICHD) that appeared in the April 25, 2001, *Journal of the Medical Association*. This national survey of 15,686 children in grades 6–10 in public, private, and parochial schools yielded some scary findings:

- One out of six students, or 16% of the surveyed students, indicated that they had been bullied themselves during the current school term.
- Almost one out of five American children, or 19%, admitted they themselves acted as bullies.
- 3.2 million children reported being victims of moderate-to-frequent bullying.

- 3.7 million children admitted to engaging in bully behaviors from "sometimes" to "several times a week."
- 10% of the children stated that they had been bullied but didn't act as bullies themselves.
- 6% of the students indicated that they were both bullied and acted as bullies.
- 13% of the students admitted that they had bullied other students but hadn't been bullied themselves.

The survey also found that bullying most often occurs in grades 6–8, and that the frequency of bullying doesn't seem to vary between urban, suburban, town, and rural areas. Males were more likely than females to both be bullied and bully. The type of bullying varied between boys and girls, with females being more verbally and psychologically bullied, while males were more physically bullied.

Other studies seem to corroborate the conclusions of this national survey. Research findings collected by the North Carolina Department of Juvenile Justice and Delinquency Violence rendered some surprising and worrisome facts about the state of and attitudes about bullying in 2000–2001:

- 39% of parents of students in grade 6 or above, and 22% of parents of students in grade 5 or lower, said that they feared for their child's safety, according to a poll taken by the Center for the Prevention of School Violence (2001).
- Bullying generally begins in the elementary grades, peaks in grades 6–8, and persists into high school (Ericson 2001).
- 74% of 8- to 11-year-old students said teasing and bullying occur at their schools (Kaiser Family Foundation and Nickelodeon 2001).
- 39% of middle schoolers and 36% of high schoolers say they don't feel safe at their schools (Josephson Institute of Ethics 2001).

Recent findings from a small local study by University of California, Los Angeles, reported that "bullying among sixth graders is a daily occurrence" (Nishina & Juvonen 2005). Nearly half of the sixth graders said classmates bullied them. The researchers studied 192 children in two ethnically diverse urban schools in the Los Angeles area over a five-day period. Students were asked to fill out written surveys describing bullying episodes that they experienced and/or witnessed each day. The study, published in the March issue of *Child Development*, reported that 62% of students at one of the schools and 42% at the other school reported that they had witnessed someone being bullied. Nishina and Juvonen were surprised: "Bullying is a problem that large numbers of kids face on a daily basis at school; it's not just an issue for the few unfortunate ones. We knew a small group gets picked on regularly, but we were surprised how many kids reported at least one incident. We didn't know how much bullying we would find over a few random days."

5

IF UNCHECKED

The Consequences

Bullying is a ticking time bomb in our schools and in our society. America needs to defuse this problem before more children are harmed, killed or take their own lives.

—Seattle Police Chief Gil Kerlikowske

If unchecked, the consequences of bullying have devastating and far-reaching effects on all children. Stressful and unsafe school environments can prevent learning; victims face anxiety and depression, while bullies may begin a life of criminal activity. Bullying doesn't touch just the victim and bully, it touches each and every student on a school campus. Its effects can last a lifetime and leave a lasting impression on all.

Unfortunately, the entire resulting harm to children is hard to measure because it is not openly shared until a tragedy occurs. Most children survive the experience, thank goodness, but with a price to pay. Experts are increasingly acknowledging that this kind of cruelty has led, and continues to lead, to an assortment of serious long-term consequences to all our children.

DEVASTATING CONSEQUENCES FOR THE VICTIM

Victims of bullying feel lonely and isolated. Unhappy and frightened, they experience school as a nightmare. Feeling unsafe and constantly worried about when the next bully attack will come, they are unable to focus and concentrate on their studies, and their grades often drop. The thought of facing a bully at school on a daily basis can literally make them sick. School phobia is a common result. Resulting from anxiety and tension, upset stomachs and headaches are also excuses (real or not, it's hard to tell) to avoid attending school.

Feelings of insecurity and low self-worth envelop the victims, who often blame themselves. Something must be wrong with them since they are singled out. They feel ashamed or embarrassed by it. Resulting poor self-esteem can lead to depression and/or violence, directed at themselves or at others, as a youth and later on. In fact, research reports that children who are bullied are five times more likely to be depressed than others, and are also far more likely to be suicidal.

The violence committed in 1999 by Eric Harris and Dylan Klebold at Columbine High School in Littleton, Colorado, shows how horrific the results of bullying can be. Twelve children and a teacher were killed, and eighteen other students were injured. The two teenage boys then killed themselves. Most observers believed this violence resulted from bullying endured by these two students over a long period of time. Apparently teased, ridiculed, and tormented, they could take no more and snapped. Here is an account of one incident they faced: "People surrounded them [Eric and Dylan] in the commons and squirted ketchup packets all over them, laughing at them, calling them faggots. That happened while teachers watched. They couldn't fight back. They wore the ketchup all day and went home covered with it."

Other similar stories with devastating consequences have filled the newspapers around the world since Columbine, including these incidents:

Canada, March 2000. Hamed Nastih, age 14, leapt off a bridge to his death. In a suicide note he described his death as the result of taunting and bullying.

Canada, November 2000. Dawn Wesley, age 14, hung herself in her bedroom. A suicide note named three girls who harassed and bullied her until she could take it no longer.

Santee, California, March 2001. Charles Williams, a 15-year-old, shot and killed two students and wounded thirteen others on a high school campus. Continually picked on and called names because he was so thin, he took revenge.

Williamsport, Pennsylvania, March 2001. Elizabeth Bush, an eighth grader being relentlessly called "idiot," "stupid," "fat," and "ugly," shot and wounded a friend who she said had turned against her and joined the others.

Tokyo, Japan, November 2001. A primary school student stabbed another to stop the taunting and physical abuse.

Canada, April 2002. Emmet Fralick was physically attacked at school on a daily basis when he didn't come up with monies demanded by a group of bullies. After selling all his belongings to pay them, he finally gave up and committed suicide.

Canada, January 2005. Travis Sleeva, age 16, committed suicide by shooting himself. He had been constantly teased about his country-style life, riding horses, and liking country music. The parents reported it several times to the school, but little appeared to be done to make it stop.

For some victims that survive the ordeal, deep emotional scars remain. Depression and anxiety disorders may continue into adulthood. According to Duane Alexander, M.D., director of the NICHD,

Being bullied is not just an unpleasant rite of passage through childhood. It's a public health problem that merits attention. People who were bullied as children are more likely to suffer from depression and low self-esteem, well into adulthood, and the bullies themselves are more likely to engage in criminal behavior.

However, some victims, who develop a distrust of their peers and have few friendships in school during the bully years, are able to turn this around later. Thank goodness that many who do receive support from family and other adults escape this severe permanent damage.

BULLYING BEHAVIORS MAY
LEAD TO CRIMINAL BEHAVIOR

As for the bully, the outlook may not be good if bully behavior patterns become habitual. Even though it may appear on the surface that bullies are popular and liked by their peers, most are not capable of maintaining close friendships over the long term. By late adolescence, their popularity begins to wane. School performance is usually weak. They are more likely than other students to get involved with drugs and alcohol as adolescents. As they approach senior high school, they are more likely to associate with other bullies and form gang alliances.

Bullying may even lead to criminal behavior. Research seems to indicate that bullying may be a first step toward serious problems later in life unless there is some kind of intervention to stop the behavior. Unless bullies learn new behaviors, they continue to bully throughout their lifetime. A study by Fight Crime: Invest in Kids, a national advocacy group made up of 2,000 police chiefs, prosecutors, and victims of violence, found that such aggression leads to serious acts of delinquency, violence, and criminal activity. "Nearly sixty percent of the boys who researchers classified as bullies in grades six through nine were convicted of at least one crime by the age of 24; 40 percent of them had three or more convictions by 24, the report said" (CNN 2003).

In another study spanning 35 years, E. Eron, a psychologist at the University of Michigan, followed children from the age of eight (who were identified as bullies by their classmates). He found that these bullies continued to bully throughout their lives. They required more support from government agencies because of a higher rate of court convictions, alcoholism, and personality disorders.

Miss America 2003, Erika Harold, herself a victim of bullying, recently helped release the report "Bullying Prevention Is Crime Prevention" (Fight Crime: Invest in Kids 2003). She said that the report and its recommendations, if implemented, "will prevent millions of young people from going through the agony of bullying, prevent thousands of suicides, and prevent thousands of kids from graduating from an apprenticeship in bullying to a graduate degree in crime and violence."

AN UNSAFE SCHOOL ENVIRONMENT
THREATENS LEARNING FOR ALL STUDENTS

What about the consequences for the rest of the students at the school? There's no doubt that learning is threatened. Every child is entitled to an education, and we have a duty to provide it in a safe environment. When the school campus is home to bullies and victims, everyone suffers. No longer are children able to do what they come to school for . . . to learn.

The good news is that finally schools are beginning to take notice. More and more schools are adopting antibully programs. This is at least a start, since research shows that at least one-half of bullying in the schools can be prevented by implementing an effective program. But the question is: have we done enough? We believe that as a nation we have only touched the tip of the iceberg. As long as one child is bullied, taunted, and harassed, we need to work harder to solve the problem. Until every school has a comprehensive program with a school-wide commitment that truly addresses the issue from all perspectives and involves all stakeholders, our children will continue to suffer.

Additionally, we need to keep the issue of bullying in the forefront, continue to research and measure bullying data, and examine the most effective programs to ensure that we bully-proof all our children.

6

WHAT CAN WE DO TO ARM OUR CHILDREN?

There is much that we can do to "arm" our children. In fact, arming our children so they do not become a bully or become the target of one is exactly the mission of this book. *Bully-Proofing Children* sets forth model climates in the home and in the school that promote antibully behaviors. An environment can be created both in the home and in the school that does not allow bully behaviors to flourish or survive. It is this antibully environment that is the secret to arming our children.

In the home, parents set the tone as caring and loving adults who are warm and accepting. They are involved with their children and continually seek opportunities to promote high self-esteem in their children. The home environment encourages open communication and the expression of feelings. Modeling and teaching the social skills of anger management, problem solving, friendship, and conflict resolution help to raise happy, healthy, and caring children, children who are respectful and able to stand up for themselves.

In the school, all staff, parents, and students are part of a school-wide commitment to create a respectful and caring environment. The staff includes teachers, principals, campus supervisors, cafeteria staff, and clerical workers. Everyone is educated as to what bullying is, why people bully, and how to recognize the players and the red flags of bullying. Rules are clearly communicated, and follow-through is consistent. All students pledge not to bully others, to help others who are bullied, and to include any students that are left out. An emphasis in the curriculum is on character education, getting along with each other, and being respectful. All adults in the school model respectful and caring behaviors.

PART 2

THE PROFILES

Who Are the Players?

The stereotypic picture that comes to mind when we think of the bully and victim is usually one of a huge, mean child picking on a small, nerdy kid. But this is often far from reality. Bullies and victims come in all sizes, shapes, ages, colors, and genders. Moreover, there are different types of bullies and victims depending on the circumstances and motivation. Understanding the players gives us a clearer understanding as to what bullying is and why it goes on. With this understanding, we are better able to address the bullying issue, come up with solutions, and build effective programs to bully-proof our children.

Bullying behavior flourishes in schools where bystanders and cliques support the bully. It's crucial to understand the role they play as enablers. Bullies are supported and encouraged by these students and often glamorized by their peers.

The actual identification of the bullies and the victims on a school campus is a very difficult task yet is crucial to eradicating bullying. Their profiles are not clear-cut. Who they are and what is happening is usually top secret. In many instances the bullies are very cautious about where and when they bully their victims. They pick times and areas in the school and parks where there is usually little or no adult supervision so they won't get caught. They threaten their victims with more harm if they should report them. The victims may be fearful of reprisals or may simply be embarrassed or ashamed to tell an adult. In some instances, the victims feel that the adult won't do anything anyway and they'll just find themselves with more problems.

7

IDENTIFYING
THE BULLY

Researchers tend to divide bullies into two types: the "pure bullies" and the combination "bully/victims." The pure bullies are children who only bully, while the bully/victims are children who bully others and are themselves victims of bullying. How and why each of them operate as bullies is very different. While in many discussions by experts, and in the findings of various studies, a distinction is not always made, it is important to understand the difference.

THE "PURE" BULLY

In a nutshell, the most common characteristics that seem to describe and at the same time motivate pure bullies are popularity and respect among their peers. They are often described as having a strong need for power and control. The feeling of empowerment is their reward. They can make someone feel bad or sad or angry. Many experts suggest that this may stem from growing up in a household where a parent was like this. This may be the accepted and imitated form of behavior.

The pure bullies rationalize in their minds that their victims deserve it. "He's a jerk and he's got too much money anyway," says the bully to his friend as he asks for John's lunch money. It's fun and a good laugh to drive another person crazy. Most bullies will respond to chastisement for their actions by saying that they were only fooling around. They will tell you that they didn't mean anything by it, that they were just looking to have a little fun. But the bottom line is that it is usually at another's expense. They care little about the feelings of others. They have little empathy or compassion for their victims.

The most recent studies seem to shatter the myth that this bully has low self-esteem and that he bullies because he doesn't feel good about himself. Most experts seem to see just the opposite. The bullies are described as popular students with high self-esteem who want respect from peers like everyone else. By pursuing others to make fun of, they feel they will earn the respect of their peers. The unfortunate thing is that in many cases they do.

THE "BULLY/VICTIM"

An increasing number of bullies that we fear and study are of the bully/victim type. These bullies have been bullied themselves. Their motivation stems from their experience as victims. The bully/victims are a lot more dangerous than the pure bully. They do not act out of a desire to simply gain power and respect from their peers but rather out of anger and revenge for being victimized themselves. Acting with this victim mentality is what may result in violence. When these victims act out their feelings and become bullies, watch out! The best example of this is the Columbine High School incident. Two teenage boys sought revenge as victims, became the ultimate bullies, and fought back violently.

Somewhere along the line the bully/victim has been bullied in the family or by peers or others. This helps explain the group of behaviors associated with them. Researchers may not call them "bully/victims" but they describe this type of bully as violent, angry and aggressive, and impulsive and lacking inner controls. These children are more likely to get into frequent fights, be injured in a fight, carry a weapon, be truant and drop out of school, drink alcohol and smoke, and vandalize or steal property.

These bully/victims may also be the bullies with low self-esteem. If in fact they have been victims, the victimization may very well have lowered their self-esteem as it created major anger issues.

IS THERE A DIFFERENCE: BOYS AND GIRLS

Though bullies come in different genders, the choice of bullying techniques between boys and girls often differs. Girls who bully also seek power and control but do it often for social advancement. Their bullying is hidden, indirect, and usually nonphysical verbal harassment. It is a hidden aggression that they express and is much harder to spot.

8

WHO ARE
THE VICTIMS?

Victims, just like bullies, come in all different shapes, sizes, and genders. There is no way that someone could walk down a hallway and pick out the victims of the school. However, the mention of the word "victim" often conjures up a certain profile. We envision a stereotypic picture of some small "nerdy" child, unfashionably dressed, walking by himself with his head hanging down. This may explain why the label "victim" has so much shame attached to it. In reality there are a variety of victims, victims who may come close to this description and victims who do not.

THE PURE VICTIM

Researchers generally point to two different kinds of victims depending on how they are targeted: the "pure" and "provocative." The pure or passive victims do little, in and of themselves, to become targets of bullies. The bullies find them. Generally, these victims do not invite attack, as do the provocative victims. Randomly, they are selected by a pure bully looking to have fun at another's expense. Usually something sets them apart, makes them the target of their peers. It may be a physical attribute or simple body language that sends a message. These victims of bullies are often smaller and somehow weaker than other kids their own age. The way they carry themselves often exudes to the observer an anxious person with low self-esteem. They may have a disability: physical, mental, or learning. Often they are social outcasts, last picked for teams and games. They may have weak social skills, be quiet and passive without many friends. The balance of power is definitely weighted on the side of the bully. These victims may become "chronic" or pure victims; victims who are repeatedly teased, when others in the same situation would not be. These victims usually take themselves too seriously and don't know how to appropriately stand up for themselves. By overreacting, they put themselves in a defensive and powerless position. Since bullies are usually careful to select their victims, usually weaker kids they know they can bully, these victims become a perfect match.

THE PROVOCATIVE VICTIMS

Then there are what we call the provocative victims. These kinds of victims may actually "egg" on the bullies by teasing or provoking them. They perpetuate the conflict but never win. Usually lacking in social skills as well, they tend to irritate and annoy their peers. Often they may be mislabeled as bullies themselves. Max, a somewhat small high schooler, was constantly bullied by not one but several students on the campus. He would make what kids would say were "off-the-wall" statements that were so annoying that the kids responded by teasing him back. Then he would yell foul. Becoming the victim was Max's way of getting attention, even if it was negative.

THE TARGETED VICTIMS

We believe that there is a third category of victims, we call them targeted victims, who deserve a separate classification and discussion. They are unlike the other two types because the bullies intentionally select the targeted victims for a specific reason. These victims have no distinct profile; they could be anyone. They can be anyone the bully has a grudge against. Among girls, it could be a beautiful girl, new to the school, who is getting too much attention from the guys. Alternatively, it could be someone with whom the bully has previously had a friendship that ended on bad terms.

These bullies are angry with their victims and act from a desire for revenge. Ironically, the bullies see themselves as innocent victims of their victims. This can be the most dangerous situation, because the bully is looking for trouble. Depending on how angry the bullies are and how quickly they get over it, their victims may or may not become chronic victims. Unlike the pure victims, their reaction may or may not be responsible for the continuation of the bullying. As much as the bullies enjoy seeing their victims get upset, their motivation for the continued bullying is the release of their pent-up angry feelings toward the victims. The James Brenton story, which appears later on in this book, is a classic example. James was a targeted victim by a group of friends who felt he had reported them to the school administration and gotten them in trouble. Once it began, the taunting and torment continued no matter what he did.

ACUTE VERSUS THE CHRONIC VICTIM

Some researchers further distinguish victims by how often they are picked on. The acute victims are only targeted once, while the chronic victims are targeted over and over again. Ironically, however, by definition, the chronic victim is the only real victim. Remember, our definition of bullying requires that the victim be someone who is repeatedly victimized. One act of teasing doesn't equate to bullying. Bullying requires repetition.

This does bring up an interesting set of questions, though. Why do some children become chronic victims after being teased once, while others don't? Why do the bullies choose to continue bullying some children and not others?

Many victims by their reactions inadvertently set themselves up to be repeatedly bullied. Their reactions serve as a reward to the bullies and keep them coming back for more. Most chronic victims will usually react by getting upset: crying, yelling or screaming, or totally withdrawing. Having clearly pushed their buttons, the bullies are happy. For bullies, who often are driven by a desire to have power and control over others, they have succeeded when they get this re-action. On the other hand, those children who are teased in the same fashion and simply let it "roll off their backs" are no fun to tease.

> Jackson, the kindergarten class bully, somehow enjoyed knocking down other students' block castles during play time. Johnny would usually yell at Jackson angrily when he did it. Jackson kept doing it to Johnny.
>
> Ashley would call other kids names during recess time. Jessica would respond calmly, "You too, Ashley." Rena on the other hand would just cry. End result: Ashley continued to bother Rena and left Jessica alone.

Training all children on how to respond to bullying can be an im-portant key to eradicating bullying, especially for the pure victims. However, it does raise an important question: Do children exhibit certain traits that make them victims, or after being teased do they become victims because of their reactions? Children who do not know how to handle bullies are at high risk of becoming victims, which would explain why these children should be armed before the bully comes along, while others are armed before the bully strikes.

9

THE BYSTANDER

Support for the Bully

In the end, we'll remember not the words of our enemies but the silence of our friends.

—Dr. Martin Luther King Jr.

I thought it was wrong to treat Sarah in such a mean way. They called her fat and told her she was ugly all the time. I felt like screaming at them when they did it, but I was afraid to because they'd start with me.

—Jessica, fifth grader

So Jessica did nothing. And Sarah continued to be bullied until she stopped coming to school. Jessica is a classic bystander to bully behavior. She probably is part of the 75–80% of students in her school who are aware of the bullying but do nothing about it. The most common reason given is Jessica's—the fear of retaliation or of being socially ostracized along with the victims. Frightened of the bullies and their friends, the bystanders unintentionally become part of the silent majority. Other bystanders report that they just don't know what to do about it so they observe quietly from the sidelines. Should they report it, it could make it worse.

If isolation is the key to successful bullying, the bystanders or silent majority by their behavior are unknowingly helping the bullies to get the victims out there by themselves where nobody will defend them. The victims are totally alone to fend for themselves. It has been argued that all bystanders are just as guilty as the bullies themselves. They may not push the victims or call them the names but, if they do nothing to stop it, they become part of it by failing to act. Bullies interpret the inaction of bystanders as approval or encouragement for their actions. After all no one is objecting to it. For the victims, this is interpreted as "everyone is against me."

THE SILENT MAJORITY CAN MAKE A DIFFERENCE

One key to bully-proofing our children is to help the bystanders, or silent majority, to speak up and make a difference. If we get this silent majority to step up and stand up for victims, bullying cannot exist. When an entire school doesn't permit it, it doesn't happen. Starting with 10 or even 20 kids courageously saying no is enough to begin making a difference. These 20 will eventually rise to the 75–80% of the school who in their hearts really do want it to stop. They may then muster up the courage in numbers to step up to the plate.

An important step is to aim to mobilize the entire school to support any and all victims. Even if we get less, it's okay. It's a beginning. Students will understand that they have the power as a group, class, or school to work together and change things—specifically to eliminate bullying as an acceptable behavior. They can make a difference. It is up to students to take a positive role in stopping it.

We need to teach our children to stand up for what is right. Understanding that it is frightening to take a stand individually, they can do it together or, at a minimum, report it anonymously to an adult. They need to learn that they, not the bully, have tremendous power because of their numbers and ability to help victims of bullying. It is their opportunity and responsibility to lend a hand.

Here is a true story of how one young man made a difference in a victim's life. This is the James Brenton story, in his own words:

What I'm here to talk to you about today is something that to this day I find a bit hard to talk about. This is because it continued to affect me for a long time afterwards and only recently have I felt able to talk about it. What I'm here to tell you about today is my own personal experience with bullying; one of the worst experiences of my life, but one which taught me a lot about myself and a lot about what needs to be done to make sure it never happens again.

A number of years ago I attended a school in Halifax, before my family and I moved to Antigonish. It was a time when a whole lot was going on, and it was kind of scary. As some of my friends began to get into trouble with the law and use drugs, I found that I was completely unready to deal with these kinds of problems. I knew that my choice was not to break the law and to never use drugs, but it was really hard to tell them that because I knew that after that we might not get along. I knew that sooner or later hanging around with these kind of people might get me in trouble.

It would happen in early February. That morning my closest friend came to the school in a fit of anger. Through a phone call from some other parent, his parents had found out about some of the trouble he had gotten into the previous weekend, and now he was permanently grounded. Understandably the boy was very upset and so he began to look around for who told on him. Everyone was asking, who had done it? Well, let's just say that it didn't take them too long to put together that I had been there the previous weekend, that I had argued against going and in the end I had decided not to take part. Gradually, more and more people began to think that it was me that had sold everyone out. I denied it when they asked, but they didn't really care what I said. They were sure that it was me.

And so it began. The situation wasn't going to end in a fight or a shoving match. Since I've always been pretty big I would have definitely preferred this. But no, they decided that there were better ways to hurt me. They decided to ignore me. Everyone decided to ignore me. But at the same time, it was more than just being ignored. This was much different. Within a week I lost all my friends and became the kind of person you just weren't allowed to talk to. Months went by this way, where no one would speak to me. Because to talk to me would mean that you were somehow involved in my supposed plan to bring down the others. So I was left entirely alone as gradually people became more open with how they felt about me. It was one day put before me by a group of students that I now had no friends and they were able to give me plenty of reasons why.

As I'm sure some of you know, there are things that can have a terrible effect on the self-esteem and confidence of a young person. I got to the point where I was always alone and never talked to anybody. I wanted nobody to talk to me because I knew it was better that way. I knew that as long as nobody talked to me, nobody could completely destroy me the way that boy and those that followed his example had. In the mornings I would leave home early and I left school late [in the afternoons] to avoid the looks and stares from everyone around me. I just wanted to be left alone.

But that is not the nature of bullying. They never leave you alone. And so it went on for months. They were always there. And I didn't do anything. What could I do? To take a stand against them would be crazy; to tell anyone, suicide. So I was left to accept it, pretending the whole time that what they thought of me meant nothing and at times it no longer did.

But one day I saw a most spectacular display, which would forever change my opinion of one person and my opinion of everyone around me. A group of boys had surrounded me, speaking of how I had no friends and why, in their eyes this was right. And that's when it would happen. A boy I hardly knew, who had been nearby came to stand by my side. He turned facing the others and in a vicious tone I'll never forget told them he wouldn't stand by and let this happen. He told them that what they were doing wasn't okay. What he said displayed a strength I sincerely doubt he really had in the face of those boys, but the very fact that he said what nobody else would meant more to me than I could possibly describe. He had completely put himself out for me and taken my side when I was weak. He helped me to see that perhaps there was some shred of decency left within certain people.

What he said that day probably only mattered to me. He never mentioned it after that day and I'm sure in his eyes it meant very little. It was just the right thing to do. But it's something I'll never forget partly because I wish I had been strong enough to say those words myself; but mainly because he was the one that saved me. He brought me back from a point where I hated everything about myself and everyone else for what they made me. I hated that I woke up every morning and hated school because I never knew how much worse that day would make it. But because of him I knew I wasn't finished yet. I would be moving soon and I could survive for another month or two. All because of some random act of kindness which meant nothing to him and the world to me.

Dr. Martin Luther King once said, "In the end, we'll remember not the words of our enemies but the silence of our friends." It's because this boy refused to remain silent that I'm here and who I am. And it has shown me that it's not the things that go right in your life, but the things that go horribly, disastrously wrong that make us who we are. Having been at the point of hating everything about myself has been a strong learning experience. It has shown me what I want to be and what I hope I'll never become.

—J. Brenton (personal communication, 2002)

James Brenton was in grade 6 at a Canadian elementary school in 1998 when this story actually happened. As a high school student he joined X-Out Bullying, a program that addresses young elementary-age students on the issue of bullying. He has visited numerous elementary schools with this group to share his experience and send the message "to never turn a blind eye to situations of bullying no matter how trivial." He currently is in college and working on bringing a similar program to the schools in his new community.

10

CLIQUES VERSUS FRIENDS

T hey are their rock, their support. Without them most bullies could not survive. The cliques are those groups of kids behind the bullies. They are responsible for perpetuating the bullying. Some of the kids participate, while others may laugh or cheer, and still others may just watch in silence. These "bully cliques" bully in groups, usually with a clearly defined leader.

Cliques may use different methods to bully. The term "relational aggression" has been coined recently by experts to describe a type of bullying behavior that "excludes others." The bullying concept is the same. The behavior (the formation of an exclusive clique) is intended to distress others and upset them. It is a power play. The others get upset because they are "left out." When children get upset at being excluded, it gives the clique that feeling of control and power. The bully wins. We see this kind of clique starting in elementary school but reaching its peak during the junior high school years.

The most well known spin on the phenomenon of cliques is the popularity clique, which seems to reach its peak also during the junior high school years. Made up of the popular or "cool" kids in the school, its members are admired and envied by others. Only a select few are allowed to join. Most other students aspire to join. But do they realize that there are rules and an image that members must conform to? In "Mr. Popularity," a short story (that follows in chapter 14) about cliques and friendship, the high price kids pay to be a member of a clique and whether it is worth it are examined.

FRIENDSHIP OR CLIQUE?

The dilemma is: If we define a clique as a small group of friends, what's wrong with that? It seems innocent enough. In life we all have our own small circle of friends because we can't be friends with the whole world, nor would we want to. In fact a group of friends is quite a supportive dynamic. But the question all kids must ask themselves is: Are these real friends?

For the purpose of this discussion, we will use the term "clique" negatively to denote a means to bully and not as a term to describe a group of friends. Thus, it becomes important for children to understand what real friendship means. Cliques exist because it is human nature to want to belong. Kids often will go to extremes to fit in and pretend to be what they're not just to be accepted. Everyone wants friends. But unfortunately members of these cliques are not usually real friends.

Examining cliques is a great opportunity for children to learn the true meaning of friendship. Certain characteristics tend to set cliques apart from friendship groups. First, the clique often is exclusive. They only let the "cool" people in and act like they are better than everyone else. Others are purposely excluded from this group. When the clique admits new members, there is often a requirement that the new member choose between them and another friend. "If you really want to be friends with us, you won't be friends with Sarah." In the clique, its members must conform and follow the rules of the group. They are often required to act, talk, and dress alike to maintain an image for the group. Members lose their identity in order to be accepted. They discourage friendships outside the clique. It is not a fun membership to hold, yet kids seek it because they are under the mistaken impression that kids in cliques are popular, cool, and happy.

Real friendship is very different. Real friends don't require each other to be something they are not. There are no rules to conform to. Real friends accept each other for who they are. They care about each other and are there in good times and bad. They are willing to share their friendship with others. Children should be encouraged to seek out real friendship and not be part of cliques. Friendships are powerful tools in kids' arsenals against bullying.

THE BULLY CLIQUE

Is a gang any different from some other types of bully cliques? Now we're discussing groups of kids that don't bully in the subtler manner described above. Rather, these cliques may roam almost like a gang with the sole intention to harass others. The lead bully has a network of others always with him or her. Bullies are basically cowards in many ways. They often need others to show off for or who will support their efforts to intimidate or harass others. They know there is safety in numbers. It's protection. It's rare that we see a successful bully not surrounded by his "troops" or the bully clique.

This type of bully clique is the worst kind that victims face. It is usually made up of students who actively join in the bullying, following their leader in teasing, pushing, or hitting the victim, or others who encourage the bully's behavior with their words or presence. They too try to act like they rule the school by intimidating, harassing, or mistreating others outside the clique. Unfortunately, other students at the school may join in against the victims to feel accepted by this power group or for fear of being targeted themselves.

There is a high price to pay for being part of either clique.

PART 3

HOW TO
SPOT BULLYING

The Red Flags

Beware: "Out of sight, out of mind."

The fact that that both the bully and victim are seeking to keep their activities and plight "out of sight," is reason enough to constantly keep our eyes open and ask questions. Just because we don't see it, doesn't mean it's not happening. All adults, including parents, teachers, and school staff, need to be on the lookout for the red flags of bullying.

Experience has shown us that children are often open to discussing this issue as long as they have a trusting relationship with an adult. In fact, I have found that they want to talk about it, but the subject in many instances is not brought up. We as adults too often are uncomfortable ourselves talking about bullying. As adults, we must not be afraid and bury our heads in the sand but rather broach the topic. If we are comfortable, so too will be the children.

Since lack of communication is one of the biggest obstacles to attacking this issue, opening up the communication gates is crucial. Developing a positive and trusting tone in the classroom and at home helps children to openly talk about any issue. Probably the best source for spotting bullying on the school campus is the kids themselves. Asking the student body is a good place to start to assess the nature and magnitude of the bullying problem. Students are usually very cooperative and will even name bullies and victims as long as it's confidential. With this information, the school is ready to start to develop an effective plan to eradicate all bullying.

11

WHAT ARE THE SIGNS?

We can't emphasize enough the importance of understanding that just because you don't witness bullying, doesn't mean it is not happening. A bully is very careful not to behave like one in the presence of adults, while victims often try very hard to keep it top secret because they are embarrassed and ashamed by it. The red flags are there but often not that obvious. As adults we need to be constantly vigilant, observing children's behaviors, watching for attitude or personality changes, and continually asking the right questions.

WHAT ARE THE RED FLAGS THAT
MAY INDICATE A CHILD IS A BULLY?

Probably the more difficult players to identify in the bully-victim scenario are the bullies, for a number of reasons. Many bullies are quite personable and hard to see in the role of a bully. Parents aren't always cooperative in accepting such a label. Behavior changes aren't always present to send up red flags as with victims. Depending on their age, the bullies may be well liked and admired by their peers and teachers. If they are a "pure" bully, unlike the bully/victim, there may be no signs apparent. In middle school the pure bullies are often the popular kids. However, in our experience, the much younger children tend to fear and separate from bullies.

Parents often don't see the red flags that could label their child a bully; after all, what parent wants to face it? Instead, they often make excuses for their child's aggressive tendencies and angry behavior. When a teacher or another parent finally confronts them, their reaction is one of surprise. Yet the whole neighborhood or school has known for years that the child is a bully while the parent is in denial mode. Research studies have shown that a bully doesn't become one overnight. Unlike the victim, who undergoes behavior changes in response to the bullying, the signs that a child may be or become a bully are present at an early age. Identifying bullying tendencies in children at a young age is therefore the best place to start, because the younger the child the easier it is to change their behavior. When children have developed a very aggressive and dominating pattern of interaction with others for a long period of time, say years, it becomes very difficult to reverse.

The most common characteristic that most experts point to, to determine if a child has bullying tendencies, is aggression. Acting aggressively can often get a child labeled as a bully. This however, may be a misnomer, if further investigation and certain questions aren't considered. Aggressive behavior can certainly be a component, but in and of itself, we do not believe this determines a child is or is not a bully. We need to look for more red flags by observing children in their play environments. Observe how they interact with their peers and parents. Ask yourself the following important questions. "Yes" answers to several questions may mean it's time to take action:

Does the child tend to dominate others and want to take control of the play activity?
Does the child have difficulty making friends?
Is the child overly aggressive with peers of the same age?
Does the child have a difficult time sharing or in general getting along with others?

Is the child quick to get angry when she doesn't get what she wants?

Does the child tease or act mean to others without provocation?

Does the child show little or no empathy and actually enjoy it when other kids get upset?

Does the child frequently get into fights with others?

Does the child use a lot of threats on his siblings and peers to get his way?

Does the child appear jealous when she is not the center of attention?

Have other parents or the school complained about the child's behavior?

WHAT ARE THE RED FLAGS THAT MIGHT INDICATE A CHILD MAY BE A VICTIM OF A BULLY?

With regard to victims, the red flags are usually there and often obvious. We haven't seen victims yet that don't unknowingly wave at least one. Sometimes they are hard to spot, depending how good an actor the victims are. Children go to great lengths to hide the fact that they are victims of a bully. They are embarrassed or ashamed and think that they should be able to handle it themselves. They may worry that if they acknowledge it or share it with others, they will be seen as weak. If they tell an adult, things may get worse and they could possibly be labeled a tattletale. So the victim generally suffers in silence.

So what are the red flags that we should be looking for to indicate that children might be being bullied? Being victimized and constantly "put down" by peers is probably the worst experience a child can go through at school. It absolutely will destroy children's self-confidence and make them feel like something is wrong with them. Victims are usually riddled with fear, anxiety, and depression and are unable to concentrate. Other kids who have been their friends may be ashamed of being the victim's friend now. Given this, it's next to impossible not to respond to this treatment and send up at least one red flag that should give the parent cause for concern. A variety of changes in behavior may constitute red flags to watch out for:

The child loses interest in school work, or grades drop.

The child doesn't want to go to school and has several reasons for this, including increasing stomachaches and headaches (15% of all school absenteeism is directly related to fears of being bullied at school).

The child seems much quieter than usual and avoids talking about school. He or she acts moody or sullen, or withdraws from family interaction.

The child seems more emotional than usual with a sad edge about him.

The child loses his appetite or may have difficulty sleeping and experience nightmares.

The child comes home from school with cuts and bruises or torn clothing.

The child has little or no interaction with others or is having a hard time making or keeping friends.

The child may have social or behavioral problems at school.

The child comes home having not eaten lunch.

The child is asking for extra lunch money because a bully is taking his lunch money.

Once red flags go up, such that a concern crosses your mind, it's time to ask yourself the right questions. Watch more observantly and open up the communication gates as described in chapter 13.

12

ASK THE RIGHT QUESTIONS

Kids Will Answer

Probably the best sources for spotting bullying on the school campus are the kids themselves. An anonymous survey to the student body is a good place to start to assess the nature and magnitude of the bullying problem. Students are usually very cooperative and will even name bullies and victims as long as it's confidential. With this information, the school is ready to start to develop an effective plan to eradicate bullying.

An anonymous survey follows with a list of questions that all students should respond to. These questions are also a great starting point for discussion of the topic in the home. Parents should feel free to raise these questions both with their child and with the school. For younger children, select the most appropriate questions and ask them orally.

SCHOOL BULLY SURVEY

For the purpose of this survey, our definition of *bullying* is any actions or words that are hurtful another. This would include when one student hits, kicks, pushes, or grabs another and when one uses words or sounds in a mean or hostile way to tease or threaten another. It also includes the spreading of gossip or rumors, behaving in a way that prevents another from joining in an activity, and trying to keep others from being another person's friend.

Directions: For each question listed below, please check yes or no to respond. Where your answer is yes, please describe and explain your answer in detail. All your answers are anonymous and confidential. They will be used to gain information *only* so we may understand bullying on our campus and plan a program to make our campus *bully-free*. No one will get into trouble as a result of this survey.

1. Has anyone ever hit, kicked, pushed, or touched you in a bully manner at school?

   _____ yes _____ no

   If your answer is yes, please describe:

   _____

   _____

   _____

2. Has anyone ever threatened you at school?

   _____ yes _____ no

   If your answer is yes, please describe:

   _____

   _____

   _____

3. Have you ever witnessed anyone being hit, kicked, pushed, or touched in a bully manner at school?

   _____ yes _____ no

   If your answer is yes, please describe:

   _____

   _____

   _____

4. Have you ever been verbally bullied or harassed?

   _____ yes _____ no

   If your answer is yes, please describe:

_____

_____

_____

5. Have you ever witnessed another being verbally bullied or harassed?

_____ yes _____ no

If your answer is yes, please describe:

_____

_____

_____

6. Have you ever bullied another student at school?

_____ yes _____ no

If your answer is yes, please describe:

_____

_____

_____

7. Have you ever been part of spreading rumors or gossip about another at school, including starting rumors or repeating them?

_____ yes _____ no

If your answer is yes, please describe:

_____

_____

_____

8. Who are the students that are the victims and get bullied or harassed? Why? Please list and explain:

_____

_____

_____

_____

9. What do you do when you see another student bullied? Do you watch, walk away, help the victim, say anything, tell an adult? Why? Please describe:

_____

_____

_____

10. Who are the bullies on our campus? Please list and explain how they bully:

_____

_____

_____

11. When and where does the bullying on the campus take place? (On the playground, classroom, hallways . . .). Please describe:

_____

_____

_____

12. Have you ever stayed home from school because you didn't want to face bullying from others?

_____ yes _____ no

If your answer is yes, please describe:

_____

_____

_____

13. Have you ever refused to allow another student to join you and your friends?

_____ yes _____ no

If your answer is yes, please describe:

_____

_____

_____

14. Do you feel safe at school all the time or just some of the time?

    _____ yes   _____ no

    If your answer is yes, please describe:

    _____

    _____

    _____

15. About how many times this school term have you been bullied by another?

    _____

16. About how many times have you witnessed another person bullied this school term?

    _____

17. What is the most popular form of bullying on the campus? Explain:

    _____

    _____

    _____

18. Why do you think kids bully?

    _____

    _____

    _____

19. What do you think you can do stop bullying?

    _____

    _____

    _____

20. Have you ever discussed bullying in class? With a teacher or another adult, including your parent?

    _____

    _____

    _____

21. What can the school do to prevent or stop bullying at school? Teachers? Principal?

_____

_____

_____

22. What can parents do to prevent or stop bullying?

_____

_____

_____

23. Does your school have an antibully policy? Describe it:

_____

_____

_____

24. What do you think kids need to learn about bullying to stop it?

_____

_____

_____

25. Is bullying bad? Why? Why not? Please explain.

_____ yes _____ no

_____

_____

_____

26. Would you like your school to be bully-free? Describe your vision of a bully-free school. What would it look like? Can we do it?

_____

_____

_____

_____

_____

PART 4

WHAT CAN YOU DO?
Antibully Solutions

Bobby, a fourth grader, was the school bully who seemed to relish teasing other boys on the schoolyard. Each day he would select one of three different boys as his victim and taunt him. Now, Nick, who was kind and nice to everyone, was selected as one of Bobby's victims because he wore rather thick glasses. Bobby loved to call him "four eyes." Nick would walk away when this happened, his head facing the ground. Bobby would laugh at Nick's response. The rest of the boys just ignored it. They were afraid of Bobby and happy they weren't one of Bobby's targets.

While it is natural to want to protect children by solving the problem for them, teaching them to solve it themselves is much more effective. As adults, when we witness or hear about children being teased or bullied, our first instinct is to "make it stop," get involved, and correct the situation. We may even feel like grabbing and shaking the tormentors and shouting "Stop being so mean. Leave him alone!" But, of course we can't do this, no matter how tempting it may be. This clearly would not help the situation. It simply would model that behavior we're trying to stop and thereby reinforce the bully's behavior.

In order to bully-proof our children, schools, parents, teachers, and pupils must work together. We must begin by opening up the communication gates so that children are willing and able to talk about bullying. The next step is to take away support from the bully by developing an effective school program. Children need to be taught how to defeat the bully and to get along with others and support each other. All students at the school must be a part of the solution. Only in this way are we able to eradicate bully and victim behaviors one child at a time.

13

OPEN THE
COMMUNICATION GATES

One of the greatest obstacles to dealing with the problem of bullying is lack of communication. Too often the issue is not openly discussed because of feelings of fear and embarrassment. Adults, whether parents or teachers, bury their heads in the sand because they underestimate the problem (maintaining the attitude that all kids tease each other) or are just unsure how to handle it, especially when they get resistance from the victim. The result is that the problem is not addressed, and bullying behaviors flourish in the resulting atmosphere of silence. It is important that all adults take this issue seriously and let children know by their actions that they will not tolerate bullying of any kind. Children need to know that they will be listened to so that they will have the courage to speak up when something feels wrong.

If bullying or teasing is part of the school's landscape, it is critical that once we recognize the "red flags," we take action. Once that "red flag" goes up, trust yourself and discuss your concerns with the child openly and honestly in a calm and unthreatening manner. Talk, talk, and talk more, keeping in mind that underneath that initial resistance, children do want to talk about their problems. It makes them feel less worried. Sometimes children need to hear stories about others with the same problem before they can "open up." Discussions at home and in the classroom (every child usually has a story) or the real-life stories in the next chapter become an effective place to start. Understanding and empathy become key to good listening.

Once the communication gates have opened and trust has been established, only then is it time to give advice to victims and practice coping strategies. It's time to confront bullies in a firm way, and let them know that their behavior is not acceptable and will not be tolerated. Classmates of the bully must learn how to take away their support for the bully, which sometimes they don't even realize they're giving.

TALK, TALK, AND MORE TALK

It's all about talking it out: whether it be child to child, teacher to child, parent to child, child to teacher, or child to parent. Talking about any topic takes away the "taboo" quality that often surrounds sensitive issues. The more bullying is discussed and addressed, the easier it gets to talk about it and consequently deal with it.

Unfortunately, a combination of factors that inhibit the parties prevent talking. Bullies are careful to hide this conduct from adults. Most bullying behaviors occur where there is little or no adult supervision. Also, victims unknowingly perpetrate the crime by keeping it a secret. Children who are victims of bullies often go to great lengths to hide the fact that they are being bullied. Initially, they don't want to talk about it. They feel isolated and alone. Feelings of humiliation or embarrassment are common among victims. Feeling that it is their fault, they may feel they did something to bring it on. They may be afraid that they will be viewed as cowardly or weak or labeled by the class as a tattletale if they say anything. Telling an adult could cause more problems or trouble for them if not handled well. Would their parents understand? What will they do or say? Will they get upset? These are all concerns that victims keep locked up.

As caretakers, we need to be proactive by creating, both at home and in school (chapter 18), an environment where bullying cannot flourish. Parents and teachers need to be positive role models by their actions. Actions do speak louder than words. Overly aggressive and heavy-handed parents often produce offspring who engage in bully-type behavior. It is important to stress and reward kindness and respect toward each other. We need to teach children about friendship, how to be assertive and not aggressive, and how to deal with conflict (chapters 20 and 21). A little prevention goes a long way.

At home, start opening the communication gates when children are very young so that when a problem does occur, they will come to you. Research indicates as little as fifteen minutes a day devoted to listening and talking with children can have remarkable results. Children who are comfortable from an early age conversing with their parents will make them their confidants when problems arise.

In the classroom, communication begins with the teacher. From day one, teachers need to make it clear to their students that they will not put up with bullying or teasing behaviors. They should begin by working with the class to set clear rules against bullying. Set time aside when students openly discuss on a routine basis how they would like to handle bully situations. Read with children. In the appendix, there is a list of books on bullying for all ages. Shorter books for young children may be read and shared in one sitting. Real-life scenarios for older children are depicted in original short stories at the end of chapter 14. These are great opportunities for children to discuss feelings, reflect on the impact of bullying on others, and learn coping strategies and friendship skills. Role-playing the parts of victims and bullies is a fun technique to help kids get an understanding of what bullying is about and why it occurs.

BE A GOOD LISTENER

Everyone enjoys being listened to. When we listen effectively, we send a message to the speaker: "What you are saying is important to me, and I want to hear you." Consequently, over time a trusting relationship is built. Conversely, when we don't listen effectively, the message is: "I don't care. I don't want to hear it." And communication comes to a halt.

If children feel that parents are good listeners, they will talk to them when things are bothering them. The question is what makes a good listener? Good listeners are those who give their total attention to the words of the speaker. They are not attending to other tasks; their eyes are focused on the speaker. Most important is for adults to believe what children tell them. Make it clear that children's reports of what is happening are accepted at face value and that they are being taken seriously. This is a crucial first step to helping children trust that you will help them with their problems. Be patient and let children tell their story in their own way as slowly as they need to.

Always allow children to express how they feel and treat their feelings with respect. Remember that feelings are not right or wrong, they are just feelings. Your response to them is all-important. Do not, I repeat, do not act upset, regardless of what you are feeling or what the child is feeling. The child is upset enough. At this point they need someone to neutralize their feelings, not intensify them. The fastest way to "shut a child down" is to respond inappropriately or fail to just listen. Some "don'ts" are necessary here, even if they seem obvious:

Don't minimize or make light of the teasing or bullying described.
Don't laugh.
Don't get angry.
Don't say, "I'll take care of that!"
Don't give advice (that'll come later).

Instead, respond in a very calm and matter-of-fact manner. Effective listening calls for asking questions and mirroring back what the child is saying. This alone will lift a heavy burden off the child's shoulders. Ask questions to gather as much information about the incident as your child is comfortable with. Ask the questions sensitively. Don't badger or interrogate. Watch for body language, eye contact, and voice tone to take clues as to how far to go. If children are getting particularly agitated, you might want to continue the discussion at a later time.

Mirroring back is a great way to demonstrate that you hear what is being said. This means repeating or rephrasing the child's words or feelings. If you start with the phrases below and finish them with the facts that are told to you, you will be using the mirroring back technique:

You feel . . .
It seems you . . .
I hear you saying . . .
You mean . . .
You believe . . .
What I hear you saying is . . .

Combining both of these listening techniques sends a clear message to children that you really care, you take them seriously, and you are "hearing" them. Below is a sample conversation with Nick, a fourth grader, which demonstrates these two listening techniques:

MOM: How was school today?

NICK (seeming a bit sad): Fine.

MOM: Did anything happen at school that you would like to talk about?

NICK: Bobby is still making fun of me, and all the other kids laughed at me.

MOM (calmly): What did he say?

NICK (upset): He called me "four eyes," and the others laughed.

MOM (matter-of-factly): The other kids laughed?

NICK: Yeah.

MOM: What other kids were there?

NICK: Billy and Jason and Mark, and they all laughed when Bobby said it.

MOM: Where did this happen?

NICK: On the playground, during recess when I struck out.

MOM: Was Bobby the only one teasing you?

CHAPTER 13

NICK: Yeah, but the others were laughing.

MOM: It sounds like the laughing by Billy, Jason, and Mark bothered you more than the teasing.

NICK: Everyone knows that Bobby is a jerk. The laughing made it worse.

MOM: Was this the first time Bobby called you a name?

NICK: No. He calls everyone names.

MOM: Was this the first time the other boys laughed when Bobby teased you?

NICK (very sad): Yes.

MOM: It sounds like it really hurt you when your friends laughed at Bobby's teasing.

NICK: Yeah.

This parent has been very careful not to say anything that could make an already anxious or sad child feel worse and at the same time has gotten all the facts. Nick, at this point, is probably feeling better because he has had a chance to "vent."

The next step is to tell children that they have done the right thing by talking about what has happened. Let children know that they are not alone and that most kids have to deal with teasing or bullying behavior at one time or another. If you remember any stories that happened to you growing up, share them now. Reassure children that it is not their fault. Do not make any promises that you cannot keep. Instead simply assure them that you are there for them and will help them resolve this, if they would like your help. Remember to explain all this to children in a way that is age appropriate.

14

LITERATURE AND REAL-LIFE STORIES HELP CHILDREN LEARN AND UNDERSTAND

Reading to or with children, or having them read stories on their own, gives them the opportunity to experience life's lessons. They can learn to relate their own life and thoughts to what is being read. At the same time, they can gain insight into themselves, who they are and what their ideas are regarding life.

Children who are bullied often feel isolated and consequently remain silent in their torture. Reading or hearing stories about others in the same situation can be comforting. Similarly, the bully, unable to step back and see his behavior from the victim's perspective, is not able to understand its effect on others and avoids communication as well. Communication needs to be opened up with both the bully and the bullied so that they can learn life's little lessons regarding friendship, kindness, and respect.

A great way to open communication channels is by using children's stories about real-life experiences with bullies and bullying to initiate discussions. Storybooks for young children such as *The Big Squeal*, *The Recess Queen*, and *Simon's Hook* are highly recommended because children enjoy and learn from them. See the appendix for additional titles.

For older kids, ages 9 to 15, the original short stories that follow are great learning tools. Names may be different, details may vary, but the plots mirror real life. They are about cliques, friendship, popularity, teasing, and bullying, which in turn is really about belonging, being recognized, and feeling powerful. The six stories have reading guides that teachers or parents may use. Each guide contains a list of thought-provoking questions about the story to stimulate discussion and make the story come alive. Select the story that is age-appropriate and addresses those bullying and friendship issues relevant to the child.

When using these guides there should be a balance to your questioning so that the child can both enjoy and learn from the story. When and how to question will depend on the individual child. Remember, every child is different. For some children too many questions will interrupt the flow of the story and can be frustrating. For other children, however, questions will enhance the experience. Let your child guide you by his reactions. Similarly, with older children be sure to make the experience both fun and enlightening at the same time.

MR. POPULARITY

I had what it takes, thanks to both of my parents—what it takes to be popular, that is. My mother was beautiful. She's still beautiful. When my mother walked into a room, people couldn't help but stare. She didn't notice it, but I always did. People liked to watch her because she didn't seem to know she was being watched. My father, on the other hand, was the go-getter of the family. He knew what he wanted and he took it. He didn't ask. He just walked away with it before anyone had a chance to protest. I was the same way. What was it, you might ask, that I wanted so badly at the age of thirteen? Popularity, of course.

I don't know if you know about this, but there is a handbook that exists. I call it the *Cool Kid's Guide to Being Popular*. You have to follow its rules or you'll be kissing popularity goodbye. Okay, it doesn't exist in real life, but it exists in the hearts and minds of all the popular kids. The rules are simple, harsh but true. First of all, you must only associate with cool kids. The people you surround yourself with must dress right, walk right, talk right, and do just enough bad things to be considered rebels but not losers. Never, I repeat, never be caught speaking to uncool kids unless you're making fun of them. Never threaten uncool kids unless you plan to follow through with it. That's how I messed up. I threatened an uncool kid and then I was pressured to follow through. See, I usually give in when it comes to pressure. Most people don't understand that about popular kids. We're the most insecure of them all. We're the ones who give in to peer pressure the quickest. We're the ones who need approval the most.

His name was Paul. He was my downfall. For some reason I hated him the moment I saw him. He was so incredibly uncool and he didn't seem to care. His clothes never matched. His hair was always unbrushed. He carried around that stupid flute case with him wherever he went. He was in the school band not because his parents forced him to but because he actually wanted to. He was the perfect target. I started laughing at him when he walked down the hallways. I started pointing him out to all of my friends. I made them laugh at him with me, but Paul never looked in our direction. It didn't matter how hard we laughed or how much we pointed. He just kept on walking, swinging his flute case. At first I thought he was pretending to ignore us because he didn't know how to handle the situation. Over time though I watched him even more carefully and I realized that he just plain didn't care that we were laughing. Just like he didn't care that his hair was unbrushed or that his socks didn't match. Paul existed in his own little world where there were no popular or unpopular kids, a world where appearances didn't matter and people didn't mind if others laughed at them. All of this made me hate him even more. I was determined to break him.

So I started watching Paul, not only as he walked down the hallway but also when we had a class together or when he was sitting at a lunch table nearby. Of course no one knew what I was doing because I was skilled at hiding things. As a popular kid I was always hiding something. Sometimes I was hiding how horrible I was feeling about myself. Sometimes I was hiding how sad I was about what was going on at home. Sometimes I was hiding the fact that I didn't really like the guys I called my friends. I couldn't hide from Paul though. He noticed, but as usual didn't really seem to care. I'm sure he thought it was strange, but it didn't appear to bother him. So I asked myself the question, does he care about anything? And that's when it occurred to me. Music. That's what mattered most to Paul. If I could somehow take music away from him then I could win.

Now all this must seem very strange to you. You're probably thinking that this obsession with hurting Paul is quite bizarre, that most popular kids aren't like me. Well you're wrong. A lot of them are. Do you know what a bottom-feeder is? See, a bottom-feeder sits at the bottom of the ocean and lives off the remains of other sea life. I've come to the conclusion that popular kids aren't much different. We feed off of what collects at the bottom in order to maintain our status. The kids that are at the bottom of the list, the ones that are considered the uncoolest, they're the ones we need the most. We tear them apart in order to build ourselves up. We need them to survive. Paul was my target. I was going to feed off him if it was the last thing I did.

So my first step was to devise a plan, a very detailed plan. It involved hurting Paul just enough so that he couldn't play his flute, twisting his arm or maybe knocking him down. I wanted him to be afraid of me. It wasn't so simple, though, because I had to worry about getting caught. The first thought that popped into my head was that I should make it look like an accident. I needed help. I needed the support of someone who was better at pulling off these sorts of stunts. That's when Tommy came to mind. He had always wanted to be my friend, but he wasn't popular enough for me to talk to him all that much. He was too much of a bad kid. He spent so much time in detention that he was hardly ever seen anywhere else. He would help me if I had a good enough reason. So I came up with one. Sure I could tell him that I made fun of Paul all the time and that he couldn't care less. I could tell him that I'd been watching Paul and giving him the evil eye and that, when he noticed, his response was to find it funny. I could even tell him about the time in math class last week when the teacher paired us up to work together and Paul requested another partner. Or I could tell him that I bragged to all my friends that one of these days I was going to get Paul. The problem was that those reasons weren't good enough.

And that's why I lied. See, this is what actually happened. My little brother, Caleb, my family's favorite, leaves a trail of toys wherever he goes. A few days before I got up the nerve to talk to Tommy, I tripped over a Lego and skinned my knee on a plastic red fire truck. What I told Tommy was that Paul intentionally tripped me when I got off the bus and then took off. I think Tommy wanted so badly to be my friend that he chose to believe me. I told him I wanted revenge. I told him that it had to look like an accident. I didn't want any traces that led back to me. Tommy just smiled in that sheepish way of his and said he'd take care of it. I felt bad when he said that. But little did I know that feeling was just the very beginning.

Now I look back and I think to myself if I had had a close friend to confide in, this probably would've never happened. If I had told anyone, anyone other than Tommy, of this plan that was forming in my head, they would have advised me against it. But, I didn't really have any close friends. Sure, I surrounded myself with people that called themselves my friends, but remember I was the most popular boy in school. All the other popular boys wanted to be me. We were always competing with each other, which didn't leave much time for friendship. If I had told a teacher or a counselor how bad I was feeling about myself around that time, this could've all been avoided. He could've made me understand that I was taking my feelings toward myself out on others. But I didn't talk to anyone because I was popular and being popular meant being perfect. Well, I was far from perfect. All of us are. And that's okay, but not if you're Mr. Popularity.

Tommy went through with it the very same day I told him what needed to be done. He went through with it before I had a chance to change my mind. It didn't go as planned for a few reasons. The reason I regret the most involves Paul's injury. Tommy was supposed to give him a minor sprain. Well, he ended up breaking his arm in two places and it took over two months to heal. The other reason it didn't go as planned was that Tommy wound up getting caught. There was a witness who helped Paul to the nurse's office and identified his attacker. Well, soon my conscience kicked in. I decided to turn myself in as soon as I saw Paul walking down the hallway with his arm in a sling and sadness in his eyes that I had never seen before. I needed to come clean. I had to apologize. The reality of what I'd done was finally setting in.

And that was that. My days of boundless popularity were over in a heartbeat. I became an outcast. Yes, I know that I deserved it, but at the same time it made me realize how useless popularity is. It's never there for you when you need it most. When I was down on my luck and I needed someone to tell me everything was going to be all right—well, that's when no one wanted to be seen with me. Tommy wound up getting detention, hours and hours of detention. As I predicted, I was the one that got expelled. They sent me to a school for bad kids, a school where no one cared what you wore or what you did after school, provided you didn't get in anyone's way. I learned quickly that none of the years I spent playing the role of most popular guy in school were helpful on this campus. We were all bad kids. That was our common denominator. Some of us were just worse than others. I was one of the few kids on their best behavior. I wanted to go back to my regular school. I knew things would never be the same. And that was okay. I didn't want them to be the same. Popularity now seemed hollow to me and hating people like Paul for no good reason seemed pointless. I wanted to go back and start over and show everyone that there's life after popularity. I also wanted to see Paul again. I wanted to ask him to forgive me, and I wanted to explain to him that I never really hated him. Some day soon, real soon, I'll get my chance.

And that's my story. Yes, I know it's a horrible one. I hope you never experience anything like it. I hope you never have to be the person who gets hurt or the person who causes someone so much pain. I hope you've listened carefully to my story. I hope you've learned from it or related to it. And next time you see Mr. and Miss Popularity walking down the hallway at your school, whatever you do, don't envy them.

Reading Guide: "Mr. Popularity"

Mr. P. realizes that popularity is not what it's cracked up to be as he discovers its "downside" and questions whether it is worth the price you pay.

Messages

Popularity often means paying a high price: changing who you are.
A bully's need for power, popularity, and respect from others often closes their eyes to the feelings of others.
Bully behavior usually loses out.
A victim who doesn't react can win in the end.

Children Learn

Popularity does not bring happiness.
A friendship is never worth sacrificing for popularity.
Popularity has an unspoken set of rules.
Never pretend to be what you are not.
Stay true to yourself.
Jealousy as a motive of the bully can make him a bully/victim.

Questions for Discussion

1. What are Mr. Popularity's rules for being popular?
2. Would you follow the popularity guide? Why?
3. What is the "price you pay" for being popular?
4. Can popularity bring happiness?
5. Why do you think it's important to be popular?
6. Why did Mr. Popularity seek Paul to make him his victim?
7. Why did Paul make him so angry?
8. Was Mr. Popularity a bully? How? Why?
9. What was meant by a "bottom feeder?"
10. How were Paul and Tommy different in their views on popularity?
11. Why did Tommy help Mr. Popularity? Would you have? Why?

LOSING BRITTANY

My name is Rubee. It's spelled funny, I know. My mom named me. She spelled it that way because she didn't want anyone else to share my name. She said I was different. I was my own person. I was independent and strong. She could tell all of that by looking at a bluish baby girl with big brown eyes and almost a full head of curly black hair. I guess she was right. I am my own person. The clothes I like no one else seems to wear. The things I say no other thirteen-year-old girl really thinks about. The books I read aren't in the young adult section.

I've been the new girl at about four different schools. Today was the most interesting "new girl" experience I've ever had because it was my first day of junior high school. It's funny how it seems like everyone is either the new girl or the new boy on campus. Some kids pretend that it's no big deal, but you can tell if you watch them close enough that it is. Even the popular kids are scared. They keep looking at one another, silently asking each other if they are acting the way junior high school students are supposed to act. The first day of school I wore white shorts, a light blue tank top, and sneakers. I didn't want to stand out too much. I admit it; I was scared. I didn't know many people. I didn't know where the classrooms were, and this time there were six of them, not just one. I also didn't really get along with the only girl I knew at my new school.

Her name was Lara. She was pretty. She dressed like the popular kids, except a little more conservatively. She got decent grades in school. She had agreed to be my friend. I'm still not sure if it was because she liked me or because we were the only girls from the elementary school across town that were going to that particular junior high school. We agreed to meet in the quad for lunch. We both brought sack lunches, even though we both knew that popular kids bought food in the cafeteria. Lara kept her lunch hidden in her backpack and snuck a bite here and there. I'll admit that I glanced into my lunch bag and felt a wave of embarrassment wash over me. It's bad enough to have to bring your lunch to school, but to have to eat the sandwiches my mother packed me, that was like social suicide. Peppers and eggs, eggplant parmesan. Hadn't my mom ever heard of ham and American cheese? She had, but we didn't eat that in our house. We were different. We were Italian New Yorkers transplanted to Los Angeles soil for the sake of Dad's new job. After the first bite of my sandwich I usually stopped caring. You can't take yourself seriously for too long. But Lara's right eye would twitch as she watched my teeth sink into a bite of green peppered eggs. I think she was afraid that someone would see me eating that sandwich and think less of her for it. That's why Lara and I don't get along very well. I get over it. She doesn't. I remember that it's just junior high school. I remember that if I don't care, chances are no one else will. Lara on the other hand thinks that everything you do is like a scar that never goes away.

Lara's not really that bad. She just doesn't understand how to handle her insecurities. It's not that I don't understand. I have those days when I question who I am too. I have days when I wish I didn't cut my hair so short, days when I wish I had a seat at the exclusive lunch table, and days when I wish I could go steady with Oliver, the cutest, most popular boy in school. The way I handle these feelings is simple. I keep my head up and my eyes focused straight ahead. I think about the things that make me happy: dance classes, my cat Simon, my grandma's spaghetti and meatballs. I try to let my insecurities roll off my back. Lara on the other hand seems to collect hers. So, I guess you could say that we were friends out of necessity. Everyone needs someone to sit with during lunch. I think we both expected that we would find other friends and leave each other behind. Lara and I didn't speak much to each other while we ate. I was too busy trying to figure out why junior high school is the way it is, and she was too busy trying to figure out why she wasn't considered one of the popular kids. We ate our lunches in silence most of the time. Actually, we did a lot of things together in silence. I didn't get a chance to mind much because a few weeks into the first semester I found out some amazing news: my best friend, who was attending a school in another district, would be transferring to my school. I knew then that everything would be all right. I found that I didn't care if I belonged to a particular group because I knew I would soon have my best friend in the world by my side. So I made friends with people I liked. Some of them were in one group, some in another; some of them even hated each other. I knew that I made people uneasy because I didn't belong to a clique, but I didn't let it bother me.

I figured there were more important things to worry about. Like my mom used to say, junior high school is just a tiny little piece in the puzzle of your life.

I remember the second semester well. I remember the first day Brittany arrived. I remember the excitement I felt upon seeing her walking down the hallway. Brittany was pretty and petite. She loved wearing raggedy jeans and her little brothers' baseball t-shirts. She had a whole collection of sneakers and cowboy boots. Everyone was always jealous of Brittany's endless selection of shoes. Brittany was different. So was I, but we were different in our own unique ways. I thought it was a match made in heaven. But junior high school is a difficult time for everyone. Bodies are changing and hormones are raging. You're on the brink of being an adult, but you're still only a kid. That confuses a lot of us. I think it definitely had an effect on Brittany. See, I thought Brittany was incapable of being confused about her identity, but I was wrong.

About a week after Brittany arrived she started searching for a place to belong. She wanted a lunch table and a set group of friends, something to protect her against the evils of junior high school. The only problem was that she expected to take me with her wherever she went. Brittany expected that she would lead and I would follow, but it usually wasn't a problem because I agreed with the decisions she made.

Brittany eventually found her place among a group of three non-descript girls: Cindy, Anna, and Jessica. I think she decided to make them her home because all the other groups intimidated her. These girls were quiet, smart, and dressed in your preppy basics. They were the kind of girls who do everything in their power to remain invisible. They don't want to be teased, so they stay out of the popular kids' way. I could understand that. No one likes to be picked on. The only problem was that Jessica couldn't understand me. She didn't understand why I had short hair or why I wore vintage dresses. She didn't understand why I had friends in different cliques. She was always making these little comments to let me know she didn't approve of me.

Jessica did approve of Brittany. Brittany knew how to act around people like Jessica. She knew how to let Jessica win every argument. She knew how to laugh at everything Jessica said even if it wasn't funny. I guess I'm too stubborn for that. It's not that I would stand up to Jessica. It's just that I would sit there quietly and not say anything. I put up with Jessica for Brittany's sake, but her resentment toward me was growing day by day. I kept trying to figure out what Brittany saw in her. She didn't have anything interesting to say. She wasn't a good listener. The only thing she liked to do was talk about herself. As for Cindy and Anna, all they seemed to do was listen to her talk about herself.

Occasionally I still saw Lara around campus. We talked about what we were up to and how our classes were. We had a lot more to say to each other now that we didn't have to hang out together every single day like clockwork. Lara had a new friend named Mindy. I liked Mindy. She always made you laugh. She had this way of making fun of things that made you feel like nothing was really that big of a deal. I think it was Mindy who first made me question why I was surrounding myself with people I didn't like much. Mindy told me interesting stories about growing up with four older brothers, she helped me solve my problems, and I offered solutions for hers. I wanted to spend more time with Mindy, not just talking in the hallways and walking home from school. Mindy made me feel how Brittany had made me feel before she started hanging out with her new friends. Don't get me wrong—I still wanted to be Brittany's friend, but I thought it might be a good idea if I wasn't around Jessica as much. I thought I could hang out with Brittany a few days a week and Mindy for the rest of the week. Brittany and I could still have our weekend slumber parties. Maybe Mindy could come sometime. Maybe we would all get along really well—or maybe not.

I think it was a Thursday afternoon when everything changed. I remember it was raining, so we hung out in the gym playing basketball instead of having to run the mile. At one point Brittany and I were both on the bench. I figured this was as good a time as any to explain myself to her. Unfortunately, Brittany's response was not as

I expected. She stood up, hands on her hips, tears in her eyes, and said, "How could you!" Then she went on and on about how if I were really her best friend I would hang out with Jessica, even though I hated her, because best friends always stick together.

That's when I realized that "stick together" meant that I should stick to Brittany wherever she goes. Why couldn't Brittany stick to me and together we could ditch Jessica? I knew why. It was because everything had to be Brittany's way. When we were younger, I never challenged her, but as I was becoming more and more my own person, I was having a harder time always doing what she said. I was also having a hard time following the unspoken rules of junior high school. The ones that say everyone must find their place at the same lunch table with the same group of kids every day. I liked different people in different groups for different reasons, and the girl I thought was my best friend didn't approve.

And that was that. I lost Brittany. As time passed I realized that I actually gained more than I lost. I gained a better understanding of myself. I felt more confident and in control. I felt better without Brittany around to tell me what to do. I also gained a better understanding of what a true friend is. Someone who really cares about you accepts that you're growing and changing, that you need to be accepted for what you were as well as for what you are becoming. Now I rarely eat at the same lunch table twice in a row. I wear what I like and I don't think twice about it. I only make friends with people like Mindy, the kind of friend who accepts you for who you are. I don't worry about approval or blending in like I did when I first set foot on my junior high school campus. Remember that nursery rhyme "Sticks and stones may break my bones, but words will never hurt me." Saying "never" is kind of an exaggeration, but if you work toward it you'll be a happier person for it.

Reading Guide: "Losing Brittany"

Rubee learns a lot about blending in, cliques, friendship, and approval at junior high school, as she is ridiculed for joining different lunch tables daily.

Messages

Believe in yourself.

It's okay to be different; in fact that is what makes each of us special.

It's good to be yourself and not conform to what others want you to be.

Don't worry about what others think, or you can never be you.

Cliques are about not being you but rather about conforming to what they require.

Children Learn

Victims let the words get to them.

They are often embarrassed and ashamed and won't talk about it.

The victim loses and the bully wins when you react.

Popularity is often about being the same and losing your individuality.

Having confidence in yourself means you don't have to worry about approval from others.

Someone else's mean words don't hurt when you accept and like yourself.

Friends are caring, understanding, helping, accepting . . .

It's up to you to choose not to be a victim.

It's up to you to choose: friends or cliques.

Questions for Discussion

1. Why was Lara having a difficult time at junior high school?
2. Who would you choose as a friend: Rubee, Brittany, Lara, or Mindy? Why?
3. Who do you think you are most like?
4. How does Rubee define friendship?
5. How was Rubee "her own person"? Was this good or bad? Why?
6. What were the unspoken rules at the junior high school?

7. Rubee didn't want to follow them. Would you?
8. Why did Rubee lose Brittany?
9. How did Rubee feel about doing what she wanted?
10. What is the difference between a clique and friends?
11. We all want to belong, or "fit in," but can we go too far trying to? Explain.
12. How did Mindy help Rubee understand what friendship was about?
13. Why couldn't Rubee be friends with both Brittany and Mindy?
14. Junior high school can be a difficult place for teenagers. Why?

THE TRUTH ABOUT MICK SLIES

His name was Mick, Mick Slies. He was tall, for a boy of fourteen. He was athletic. He got good grades without trying. He also had this mischievous gleam in his eye that attracted almost all of the girls' attention. To top it all off, he was more interested in skateboarding than he was in finding himself a girlfriend, which made the girls even more eager to win him over.

Candace was one of Mick's many admirers. She was a petite girl with long red hair and dark green eyes. She stood out in a crowd not only because of her unique coloring but because she dressed differently than your average teenager. Her mother was a clothing designer and so she was always on the cutting edge of fashion. Candace, however, was not so unique in the way she behaved toward Mick. She eyed him obsessively, wrote his name beneath hers on notebooks, and knew exactly where to run into him in between classes.

Lane was Candace's best friend and she was equally obsessed with the one and only Mick Slies. She was more discreet about it than Candace, but there was no denying her fascination with the blue-eyed boy wonder. Lane wasn't bold enough to write his name in hearts on her notebooks, but she was smart enough to sit next to him in the classes he didn't have with his friends. That way when their math teacher, Mr. Riley, asked the students to pair up into study groups, she could immediately offer to be Mick's partner. Candace and Lane's friendship seemed close to perfect except for Mick. Mick was the only sore spot. Candace thought that because she had spotted him first, Lane should back off. Lane thought that because she was on speaking terms with him and Candace wasn't that Candace should be the one to leave him alone.

Then of course there was Mick. Not the Mick that the two girls dreamed about, but the actual Mick, the Mick that wasn't as ideal as Candace or Lane thought him to be. It was true that Mick was more interested in skateboards than girls, but that didn't mean he wouldn't pretend to be interested for the sake of impressing his friends. This was the side of Mick that his admirers were unaware of. This was also the side of Mick that made him popular among the boys. Not only could he get all the prettiest, most popular girls to like him, but he could also tell endless stories about them in the locker room, stories that all of his friends could laugh at. Mick wasn't looking for a girlfriend; he was looking for a girl to make fun of. Why couldn't Candace and Lane see through Mick Slies? For that matter, why couldn't any of the girls at Mercer Junior High see him for what he really was? Well first of all, they didn't want to see it. They wanted him to be something he was not. Second of all, each of his admirers was convinced that she could change him. She would manage to make Mick like her more than sports and skateboards. She could make Mick like her so much that he would never think of talking behind her back.

Then there was Randy. Randy was friends with both Candace and Lane. Maybe not friends, but close acquaintances. Randy attended Mercer Junior High School, but Candace and Lane rarely said hi to him when they passed him in the hallway. It's not that they were ignoring him. It's just that Randy was the kind of boy who was often overlooked. Randy wasn't overweight, but he wasn't in shape either. He hated sports and loved to read. Randy didn't care much about his appearance. He wore one of two pairs of jeans everyday and old t-shirts advertising places that didn't exist anymore.

Randy had one close friend, Stew. Stew was the class nerd, the smartest boy in school, who was unlucky enough to have to correct his vision with the kind of glasses that make your eyes look too small for your head. Randy loved Stew because he could relate to him. They would sit for hours talking about things that most fourteen-year-old boys have no interest in. Randy's father owned the local convenience store. After school Randy would sit behind the counter reading or doing homework. His dad needed the free time to stock new shipments. That's how Candace and Lane knew Randy. They would stop by the store on their way home from school to buy snacks with their leftover lunch money. The girls were friendly with Randy but they didn't think twice about him or they didn't let on if they did. What was it about Randy? It's hard to say, but there was something about him, a quality that had nothing to do with being cool or popular. Maybe it was intelligence or kindness. Maybe it was carelessness or acceptance. Whatever it was went unnoticed by Candace but not Lane. And Randy—well, Randy knew that Lane noticed.

Who could forget about Mick though? Mick, the boy who was so cool he almost didn't seem real. The girl who could win Mick Slies's heart would be, without a doubt, the reigning queen of popularity. Lane couldn't trade in her hopes of one day walking hand in hand down the hallway with Mick for someone as plain and unpopular as Randy—or could she? If she wanted to keep the majority of her friends she knew she couldn't.

When Lane and Candace would walk into the EZ Mart around 3:45 P.M., Randy would be reading a book by some author whose name neither of them could pronounce. His face would light up when Lane walked through the door. She just smiled and politely said hello. So did Candace. While the girls were paying at the counter, the three of them would talk about teachers, students, homework they liked and didn't like. See, it wasn't that Randy was unpopular; he was just nonexistent. It was safe to talk to him. His friendship would not elevate your status in the eyes of the popular kids, but it wouldn't cause you to fall out of good graces with them either. It was safe to think Randy was a good guy, but to actually like Randy—well, that would be a whole other story.

And so Randy remained nonexistent and Mick maintained his heartthrob status until one fateful day when Randy said too much.

It was a day like any other day. Randy sat behind the convenience store counter breezing through his math homework. The bells hanging on the handle of the front door jangled. In walked Candace and Lane in particularly high spirits because today was the first day of a four-day weekend. Randy glanced up and smiled. The girls waved and headed straight for the ice cream cooler. Tonight they were having a slumber party: 12 girls, sleeping bags, cheesy movies, popcorn, and ice cream. Candace's parents were out of town for the weekend and they had agreed to let her have this party provided her older sister Lana chaperoned the festivities. The girls went back and forth between mint chip and cookies and cream before deciding to just get both flavors.

Candace and Lane approached the counter. Randy put aside his book. "What are you guys so excited about?" he said.

"I'm having a party—a slumber party," said Candace. Then she laughed because Randy's eyes were focused on Lane even though she was talking. Sometimes Lane didn't say much around Randy. Sometimes Randy made her nervous, but nervous in a good way. Lane glanced down at her shoes thinking her cheeks might be flushing red.

Randy quickly shifted his attention toward Candace. "So what exactly goes on at those slumber parties?"

Candace smiled mischievously at Lane. "Should we tell him?"

"Like it's a big secret," said Lane quietly.

"We watch movies and eat junk food, but mostly we talk. We talk about boys. Well, we talk about one boy. It's so stupid how we all like the same person," said Candace.

"Who's the lucky guy?"

"You don't know? Oh my God. Everyone else knows. It's probably 'cause you always have your nose in a book that you never noticed," said Candace. "It's Mick Slies."

Randy's playful smile dropped. Candace continued playfully. "You thought I was gonna mention your name, didn't you?"

"Yeah right," laughed Randy. "I guess of all the people it could be, I was hoping it wouldn't be Mick."

"Why would you say that, Randy?" Lane's curiosity was peaked.

CHAPTER 14

If Candace had asked, Randy probably wouldn't have answered her. Randy didn't like to gossip much. He figured if you had something to say, you ought to just say it to the person's face. It was Lane, though. The way she looked at him questioningly, the way she said his name opened the floodgates. He spilled the beans.

Randy told them all the things they probably didn't want to hear. He told them how cruel Mick was, how he told stories behind people's backs in order to make the boys laugh. He told them how he rated all the girls on what he called "the ugly scale." He also told them he talked about the girls he thought were easy.

Candace was shocked. Lane was too, but less so. Candace kept on saying how she couldn't understand why he would do something like that. Randy explained it to her. He said that Mick made fun of the girls so that other boys would like him and so that they wouldn't be jealous that these girls liked him instead of them.

Lane looked relieved to learn all of this. It was as if she had known it all along and just needed to have someone remind her of it. Candace on the other hand was devastated. It was like someone had just told her the tooth fairy wasn't real. Randy was confused. Part of him felt like he shouldn't have said anything. Part of him felt like they had a right to know. On their way out, Candace thanked Randy for telling them the truth about Mick. The thank-you wasn't all that convincing, probably because her disappointment was showing through. Both girls said goodbye and headed toward the door. Lane glanced back over her shoulder thinking it's too bad there aren't more people like Randy in this world.

The slumber party was almost a success. The choice of movies was perfect. The ice cream seemed to disappear in a matter of minutes. Everyone was happy and full of laughter. Even Candace seemed to have forgotten about the conversation with Randy earlier in the day. But then someone mentioned the most popular boy in school and before Lane could stop her, Candace was relaying the truth about Mick Slies.

Lane cringed. She knew it was a bad idea. Randy had told them this in confidence, and here Candace was sharing the news like it made headlines in today's newspaper. Of course as the story came to a close, Candace had 12 very disappointed girls on her hands. There was no more ice cream to eat and no more movies to watch. The rest of the night was supposed to be devoted to talking about the boys they liked or, rather, the boy they liked. Sadness eventually turned into denial. Several of the girls didn't want to believe that such a story was true. They had to know who told Candace and Lane all of this. They had to know if it was a reliable source. Now it's not that Candace was cruel, but sometimes she spoke without thinking about the damage her words might do. As soon as the question popped up, Lane furiously shook her head no. Candace didn't exactly ignore Lane but she didn't pay her much attention either. She went right ahead and identified Randy. That's when Lane jumped in and begged the girls not to let Randy's name leave the party. No need to get him in trouble for letting the information leak.

That was when the teasing started. Why was Lane so concerned about Randy? Everyone wanted an answer. Lane, of course, denied that she cared. She said she just didn't think it was fair to get him in trouble considering he was nice enough to tell them what he knew. The girls didn't buy that as an answer. They continued making fun of Lane until she appeared visibly upset by it all. That's when they all agreed to keep everything to themselves and not drag the gossip to school on Monday.

Unfortunately, asking 12 teenage girls to keep a secret is like asking a balloon with a hole in it not to leak. No one knows who told, but everyone knows someone slipped up. What probably happened was one of the girls who was at the slumber party told someone who wasn't there. She must have prefaced it by saying, "You have to promise not to tell anyone." Then that person most likely told someone else the story by prefacing it with, "You have to promise not to tell anyone I told you." The information must have continued on down the line and eventually reached someone who decided to tell the truth about Mick Slies to Mick himself. As soon as Mick heard the news that was circulating around school, he did what every respectable popular boy is supposed to do: He threatened to beat someone up. In this case, the someone turned out to be Randy. Randy took the news fairly well. He found it funny, but he was smart enough to know not to laugh out loud at it.

Instead, he simply refused to fight Mick. He didn't care that everyone was calling him a wimp and laughing or pointing when he walked down the hallway. He thought fighting was pointless and that it didn't really accomplish anything.

It's amazing how your junior high school status can change in a matter of days. It's strange how people you don't even know can start hating you because you said the wrong thing about one of the popular kids. It's ridiculous how you can become the butt of every insulting joke that makes its way across campus simply because you believe trading punches with someone is pointless. And so Randy made his way from nonexistent to social outcast quickly and quietly. He didn't say anything to Candace and Lane about the situation. He couldn't even if he wanted to because they hadn't been in the store lately and they tended to walk the opposite way when they saw him coming down the hallway. That's what bothered Randy the most. Not the hoards of kids deciding they didn't like him when they didn't even know him. No, it was Candace and Lane. He had helped them out, and now they were turning their backs on him. That figures. At least, that's what Randy kept saying to himself until the front door jangled and Lane slid in looking overwhelmingly shy and embarrassed. She didn't proceed to the candy aisle or the ice cream cooler as per usual; she headed straight to the counter.

"I'm sorry." The words popped out of her mouth like a small explosion. She turned around and headed back toward the exit.

"Wait," said Randy. Lane stopped dead in her tracks. "Do you want to—to sit with me awhile?"

"Sit with you awhile?" Lane's voice wavered ever so slightly.

"I think you're answering a question with a question," laughed Randy.

"Am I?" said Lane. Then they both laughed, and Lane didn't seem to mind that her cheeks had blushed red.

Lane and Randy continued talking for several hours. Lane felt comfortable around Randy, as she did with her close friends. He was funny and he had interesting things to say. Most importantly he made her feel special, unlike Mick, who made her feel like she was one of many. And so that afternoon sparked several changes, changes for the better. Lane left the store hoping to see Randy the next day at school. She wanted to be around him. It didn't matter how it affected her social status. Randy made her feel like popularity was an old jacket she had grown out of. If the popular kids had a problem with her spending time with him, well then so be it. All easier said than done, right? Not exactly. Sure, some of Lane's friends didn't want to have anything to do with her once she started hanging out with Randy. But that goes to show you that they weren't really her friends in the first place. A true friend likes you for you, not just for how popular you are. In a sense Randy allowed Lane to sift through her friendships and figure out which ones were real and which were not.

Of course Candace and Lane remained friends. Candace was loyal to Lane. She stood up for her when other girls made fun of her for liking Randy. She also spent time with both Lane and Randy. Somewhere along the way, Randy helped her to see that she didn't have to like the most popular boy in school simply because he's the one who's the most popular. As for Mick Slies, he eventually gave up on Randy. He was getting nowhere fast, and the situation was looking more ridiculous every day. That's not to say that Mick's social status changed dramatically. He was too popular to be dethroned simply because Randy told the truth about him. In fact, the rumors about Mick faded fast, and he had girls following him around again within a few weeks. See, some people learn their lessons the easy way; they only have to be told once. Others learn their lessons the hard way; they trip over the rock someone just told them was in their way. In the end though, it's learning and growing that counts.

Reading Guide: "The Truth About Mick Slies"

Popularity isn't worth the sacrifice of giving up who you are.

Messages

Don't judge a book by its cover.
Don't try to be what you're not.
Friendship is a special bond that is hard to break.

Friendship means accepting others for who they are.
The only approval that you need is your own.

Children Learn

What's inside a person is more important than what is outside.
Real friendship embraces loyalty, caring, and understanding.
Popularity often strips us of who we are.
Stay true to who you are.
Being cool is being you.
Friendship is more precious than being popular.

Questions for Discussion

1. What was the "truth about Mick Slies"?
2. Did you like Mick Slies? Why? Why not?
3. Would you have liked to be Mick's friend? Why?
4. What did Candace and Lane learn from the truth about Mick Slies?
5. Describe the relationship between Candace and Lane? Was it a friendship? How so?
6. How did Randy handle Mick's bullying? Did it work?
7. Why did the kids turn their backs on Randy? Do you think it was right?
8. Do you think Randy was wrong to tell Lane and Candace about Mick?
9. Why did Lane apologize to Randy in the end?
10. Do you think kids like kids only because they are popular? What about you?
11. What did you learn from the story?

THE SEA WORLD INCIDENT

Jane Dahl is simple, like her name. She is average height, fair-skinned, and plain. She is not exactly overweight, but she is not at her ideal weight either. Some of the kids in school ignore Jane, but most of them make fun of her. Of course there is nothing particularly worthy of making fun of in Jane, but someone has to be the victim of cruel junior high school jokes.

Marley Swanson is almost too pretty to be a junior high school student. Awkwardness somehow passed her by and she knows it. She never had to contend with acne or the extra weight that most preteens put on. Marley is the second most popular girl in school. She has everything that the most popular girl has, but she behaves in school, unlike Sandra, who cuts class and steals cookies from the lunch line.

Sandra is the most popular girl in school because she acts as if she is better than everyone else and pretends that rules do not apply to her. She makes fun of people she thinks are uncool and she only lets certain people sit at her lunch table. Marley was selected to sit next to Sandra at that table. Sandra just decided one day that Marley was going to be her best friend. Marley already had a best friend who went to another school, but no one says no to Sandra.

Most people think Marley has it all. She is one of the prettiest girls in school. She is best friends with the most popular girl in school, and she manages to get decent grades even though she hangs out with the cool crowd more than she studies. But Marley isn't happy and she was particularly unhappy on the day she started making fun of Jane Dahl. Jane never sat next to Marley on the bus. Popular kids only sit in the back with other popular kids. It is an unspoken rule. Well, one day Jane and her mother were running late. They barely made it to the bus on time. As Jane stumbled through the bus door, she realized there were no more seats at the front. The only seat left was in the back, the very back, and half of the seat was already occupied by Marley Swanson.

As Jane made her way down the aisle she held on tightly to her books. She could feel beads of sweat forming on her brow. She wished her mother had been running just a little bit later so that the bus would have left without her. She wished that she were thinner and prettier and didn't get straight As so that the popular kids would accept her with open arms. She moved slowly, hoping that the bus would somehow make it to school before she made it to the seat in the back of the bus. Jane sat down quietly next to Marley. Maybe Marley wouldn't even notice she was there. But Marley did notice and so did Sandra. Marley might not have said anything had Sandra's eyes not been encouraging her to. Marley glanced back and forth between Jane and Sandra. If she didn't say anything, Sandra would never forgive her. She would take back the friendship charm and the best seat at the lunch table. Popular kids make fun of unpopular kids whenever they have the chance. If Marley failed to say something to Jane, the popular kids would doubt that she belongs with them.

"This isn't Sea World." The words spilled quickly out of Marley's mouth. Jane just sat there as silence fell all around them.

"Whales don't belong here," spat Marley. Jane felt her cheeks flush bright red as the bus erupted with laughter. There was nowhere to go, no one to help her. The few friends she had were just as scared of the popular kids as she was. And so Jane sat quietly trying to force her tears to run inward.

After the "Sea World incident," both girls were never the same again. Jane never used to miss school. She was the girl who received the attendance award every year, that is until she started hoping to catch every cold and flu that circulated around school. Sickness was like a gift. It meant Jane could stay home from school. Marley also changed. She never used to make fun of the unpopular kids. She was the quiet one of her group of friends. But Marley liked the attention she got when she made fun of Jane. She wanted more of it, so she teased Jane every chance she got. Pretty soon everyone was calling Jane "the whale."

On an exceptionally hot day, all the popular girls were dressed in jean cut-offs and flower-print tank tops. Jane wore pants and a long-sleeve shirt, hoping she could somehow hide beneath her clothing. Sweat trickled down the back of her neck. The popular girls would make fun of her if they noticed. She prayed that day would be different. It was Jane's birthday.

"Got you a present." Jane turned around, startled to see Sandra hovering behind her with her hand extended. "Take it." Jane sat there quietly. Sandra dropped a small key chain onto her desk. Jane examined it. The paint is chipped, but you could still tell what it was. It was a plastic circle with a small gray whale on it.

"Happy birthday," laughed Sandra, as giggles erupted from the rest of the class. Jane's cheeks turned red, her eyes welled up with tears. She couldn't stop them from dripping down her face. Sandra glanced over at Marley. Why wasn't she laughing? Marley felt Sandra's eyes on her. She laughed. She had to laugh, or everyone would think she was on Jane's side. Marley thought Sandra sometimes took it too far, but she was afraid to tell her, so she giggled along with everyone else. Once Jane's legs could carry her again, she stood up and walked toward the door. The teacher kept calling her name, but Jane couldn't hear her. She only heard the laughter. Jane sat in the bathroom for the next two hours, waiting for the bell that signaled the end of school.

"Hey there, birthday girl," said Jane's mother as Jane slid into the car. "How does it feel to be 13?"

"Same as it did to be 12," replied Jane.

Jane's mother, Martha, shrugged off the negativity in Jane's voice. She must have been kidding. But Jane was not kidding. She felt just as miserable at the age of 13 as she did at the age of 12. The feelings of loneliness and insecurity that Jane had to deal with in school were with her when she left school. It didn't matter if she was spending the day with her mother or sitting in her bedroom by herself, she still felt like there was a group of kids around her making fun of the way she looked and acted. Jane glanced over at her mother, Martha. Martha was not thin; she was curvy but it suited her frame. Her long blond hair was pulled back in a French twist. She wore just enough makeup to enhance her bright green eyes. Jane wished that she could wear contacts like her mom instead of thick-rimmed glasses, and then maybe everyone at school would notice that she too had beautiful green eyes.

Martha glanced over at Jane. She thought back to when she was in junior high school. She also went through an awkward stage, a time when her peers picked on her—not as frequently as Jane, but enough to remember it well. If only Jane would tell her mother about what happens at school, Martha could tell Jane stories that would comfort her. Martha could explain to Jane that it gets better as you grow up and grow into yourself. But Jane refused to tell her mom how she felt because she was embarrassed. They drove on in silence. Martha and Jane drove along the same road they always drove to their light blue house with the white picket fence. Jane looked at her mother questioningly when she turned off that road and onto a busier street.

"I have a birthday surprise for you," said Martha. Jane tried to force a smile even though she would rather go home and forget that today was supposed to be her special day. Martha hung a right into a strip center parking lot. In the far corner sat Sally's Sundaes, their final destination. Jane slumped lower in her seat. Of all the places to have ice cream after school, why did her mom have to pick the one place kids from her school liked to hang out on hot days? Jane almost protested, then she remembered that her mom probably would not understand anyway. Martha parked her tan-colored minivan in front of the ice cream parlor. A few kids stood outside the double glass doors, but they were high school kids that did not know Jane as the class whale. They entered Sally's and headed toward a small table that had colored animal balloons attached to each chair. Robert, her father, occupied one chair; Sammy, her little brother, another; and Aunt Dottie, her mother's younger sister, a third. Robert was tall and thin, a good-looking man in a pin-stripe suit. Sammy looked just like his father, except he was only ten. As for Aunt Dottie, she always brightened Jane's days. Her jeans were always torn, and paint always decorated her t-shirts and sometimes her face. Aunt Dottie painted beautiful mural-size paintings and never changed out of her painting clothes after a hard day's work. Jane thought Aunt Dottie was the most beautiful woman in the world, beautiful in her carelessness. Robert ran over to his daughter with open arms. Jane could not help but smile even though she was a bit embarrassed to be the center of attention. Sammy spat a wad of paper through a straw at her, his special way of saying happy birthday. Aunt Dottie just winked and ruffled her hair. Jane had stood in front of a mirror several times to practice winking like Aunt Dottie.

In front of one of the empty seats at the table sat the Kitchen Sink, a sundae of enormous proportions. "That's your seat, kiddo," said Robert with a smile. Jane sat down in front of the ice cream, forgetting how horrible the earlier part of her day was. Time passed and Jane began to feel like today *was* her special day.

Her mom and dad knew Jane well enough to give her spending money so that she could pick out her own presents. Aunt Dottie gave Jane a set of oil paints and some blank canvas so she didn't have to borrow them from her anymore.

Then the door opened and Jane's heart stopped. At least she thought it stopped. In walked Sandra and Marley accompanied by Jackie, Michael, James, and Hilary. Jane bowed her head in midbite, hoping they wouldn't notice, but the multicolored animal balloons tied to the chair gave her away. As the ice cream in Jane's stomach rose into her throat, Marley glanced at Jane. She quickly looked away. Relief washed over Jane. Then Sandra noticed the party table, the balloons, the family, and Jane at the head of it all. Sandra continued to stare, a smile creeping over her face. She stared long enough to prompt everyone she was with to turn and look at what she was staring at. Sandra laughed loud enough so that her friends could hear, soft enough so that Jane's family couldn't.

"I—I have to—to go to the bathroom," stammered Jane. She stood quickly, knowing that she would have to pass by her enemies in order to get to the bathroom, but at this point she couldn't care less. She had to get out of their line of vision, even if it was only for a moment. She had to regroup. She couldn't let her family know she was the laughingstock of her junior high school. Jane sang her favorite song in her head as she passed by Sandra, hoping that the lyrics would drown out whatever Sandra had to say to her. But at the moment Jane was a few feet away from Sandra, she suddenly forgot her favorite song; she forgot all her favorite things.

"Do you really think you should be eating that sundae? It's gonna go straight to your whale gut." Sandra was pleased with her attack.

The boys were laughing hysterically, the girls were giggling. Jane stopped dead in her tracks. She had never stopped before. It seemed like she was always passing by or running by or trying to get away from something.

The tears ran down Jane's cheeks, before she even had a chance to think about them. She looked Sandra straight in the eye. "It's my birthday! Could you just let me have *one* day. One day you *don't* make me feel like I wanna die!" The boys laughed, but it's uncertain at whose expense they are laughing. Jackie and Hilary laughed at Jane, calling her a crybaby and knowing if they did not take Sandra's side there would be hell to pay later. Marley stood there quietly not knowing how to handle to situation. Her heart suddenly hurt, but she figured when in doubt do nothing.

Jane turned around and headed back to the party table, knowing she would pay for her outburst but feeling relieved that she stood up for herself. She quietly asked her mom if they could continue the party at home. Everyone took the cue and headed toward the door. Aunt Dottie slowed her pace. She let the rest of the family exit and then she called over to Sandra and her friends, "What goes around comes around. You can't treat people like that and get away with it. Eventually it'll come back to haunt you. Not tomorrow, but when you least expect it."

"Whatever," replied Sandra nastily. Marley laughed to herself, thinking how stupid Sandra sounded. Aunt Dottie exited and Sandra looked flustered for the first time in a long time.

Jane woke up the next morning, forgetting the sadness of yesterday's incidents. She glanced at the stack of presents that sat in the corner of her room. She noticed her new oil paints and remembered how easy it was for Aunt Dottie to stick up for her and how difficult it was for her to stick up for herself. As Jane headed toward the bus stop, she expected to feel an overwhelming sense of dread. Instead she somehow felt lighter, like a weight had been lifted off her shoulders. She did not care as much. She was accepting that her social standing in school might not be as important as she once thought it was. There was a whole other world out there, a world where people like Aunt Dottie told off people like Sandra and Marley. One day Jane would be a part of that world. She would leave behind her seat at the front of the bus, her exclusion from the popular lunch table, and the teasing remarks that followed her down the hallways. One day Jane would forget all the popular kids' names and they would forget hers, nickname and all. With this kind of outlook, the day couldn't help but go smoothly.

It was an especially good day for Jane in Spanish class when she received the highest score on a test she had struggled with. It was a horrible day for others though. Mrs. Ramirez was holding two stacks of papers, shaking them angrily in the air. She couldn't understand how half the class could pass with flying colors, while the other half failed miserably. The answer was simple: Some students had decided that they had better things to do than study. Mrs. Ramirez had a simple solution for this problem.

"We're dividing up into two groups," said Mrs. Ramirez. "Those of you who chose not to study go to the right side of the room. Those of you who did study go to the left. Then you're going to find your-self a partner, a tutor from the opposite side of the room. The tutors will receive extra credit. Those being tutored will get a chance to re-take the test."

Everyone got up and moved about the room. Jane expected to sit alone, until it was down to the last unpartnered person. It did not bother her as much today. She sat quietly, patiently waiting for an-other person who was equally as unpopular as she was. She heard footsteps approaching behind her. She turned around expecting to find Daphney or Stewart, her fellow outcasts, but instead it was Mar-ley walking hesitantly toward her.

Marley did not exactly know what she was doing. Something in-side of her propelled her forward. Every time her father told her she's not good enough and why couldn't she be more like her sister, she felt that feeling Jane spoke of in the ice cream store. Suddenly she couldn't understand why she ever wanted to make Jane feel like her father made her feel, like she wanted do die. Maybe not die, just disappear forever.

"Hi," said Marley. For some reason all other words escaped her for the moment. Jane stared at her questioningly, forcing her to continue. "Do you, uh, wanna be my partner?"

Jane assumed this was the beginning of some practical joke. It always was. She quickly declined the offer.

"Please. I need your help," said Marley. "Not in Spanish class. Well yes in Spanish class, but also—oh god. Never mind." Marley's cheeks flushed with embarrassment.

"Please, Marley, not today."

"You don't understand. I'm not like them. I'm like you. They just think I'm like them 'cause I pretend I am. I guess I wanted to say sorry. That's all."

"If this is the beginning of a practical joke," said Jane, "it'll be the meanest one yet. Sit down."

Relief spread across Marley's face. Sandra's jaw dropped as Marley and Jane pushed their desks together. The girls knew they would both have to contend with Sandra, but then again everything was easier when you had a friend to help you through it, and they had each other. Marley could tell Jane was willing to forgive her.

After that day in Spanish class, things changed once again for both Jane and Marley. Marley did not become the most unpopular girl in school, but she lost her seat at the lunch table. Jane did not become one of the popular kids, but the teasing started to fade away. Marley did not spend so much time shopping at the mall. She started studying more. Jane did not spend so much time alone in her room. She started hanging out with Marley on weekends. Jane had never had many friends. She was grateful to finally have someone to confide in. Marley had always had plenty of friends, but she never confided in any of them. She was grateful to finally have a friend she could trust. That first year of junior high school came and went, and Sandra just became a bad memory for both of them. In fact, right before summer vacation started, Sandra got expelled from school for stealing a teacher's wallet. By the time they started high school both girls had practically forgotten her name. Jane and Marley, on the other hand, remember each other well because they have remained, and always will remain, friends.

Reading Guide: "The Sea World Incident"

This story focuses on the dynamics of bullying and the cruelty of bullies as they seek to harass children who are different in order to feel powerful.

Messages

> Kids bully others to feel powerful.
> The victim, ashamed and embarrassed, suffers in silence and feels isolated.
> Bystanders often laugh because they are supposed to, or are afraid not to, and unwittingly support the bully.
> Kindness and friendship are more important than popularity.
> Treat others the way you want to be treated.

Children Learn

> Bullies don't care about others' feelings. They have no empathy.
> They act to empower themselves.
> The reward is control over another.
> Kids join in on bullying so they can belong.
> It's important to reach out to others . . . being ashamed makes a victim the perfect target.

Questions for Discussion

1. How does Marley change, and why?
2. How does Jane feel after she stands up for herself? How does she change? Why?
3. How does Jane change by the end of the story? Why?
4. Why did Marley initially start teasing Jane? Why did she keep doing it?
5. How did Jane feel? How would you have felt? Handled it?
6. What finally made Marley look at things differently?

7. Have you ever treated anyone, or have you been treated like that? Do you know anyone who has?
8. Why didn't Jane tell anyone? What would you have done? Why?
9. Do you know anyone like Sandra or Marley? How so?
10. How did Jane feel about herself?

THE FRIENDSHIP TEST

There were once two boys who were instantly drawn to each other. One boy's name was Marc, the other's Sam. Marc and Sam became best friends the first day that Sam arrived at Lockwood Elementary School even though both boys had lived very different lives up until Sam moved into Marc's quiet, small-town community.

Marc had actually spent almost every day of his life in Lockwood. His mother and father lived in the city when they were young and free of financial responsibilities. But a year after he was born they moved to Lockwood because his father felt it was a better place to raise a family. Not much changed for Marc's father, except for the distance he had to commute to work. He still stayed in the city after work and had drinks with his buddies, who were single and didn't have families yet. He came home to his dinner sitting on the counter covered in tin foil, Marc and his mom having long since turned in for the night. Everything changed for Marc's mom. When Marc was very little his mom used to glow. There was a vibrancy about her that affected everything and everyone around her. Marc had long since forgotten when he first noticed the sadness collecting in her eyes. He had forgotten that it all began when they moved to Lockwood and Marc's mom gave up her hopes and dreams of becoming a singer.

When Marc's mom was taken away and put in the hospital, Marc figured that it was his fault. After all, he could hardly ever make his mom smile. He was too young to understand what cancer was. He thought his mom was dying of a broken heart. It was only a matter of months before Marc's family consisted only of his father, his little brother, and himself. Now that mom was gone, Marc thought that dad would step up and fill in. He didn't. He hired Esmerelda to take over mom's duties and stayed in the city even more often.

Marc had experienced all of this by the ripe old age of nine. He was clearly different from your average nine-year-old boy. He was quiet and thoughtful. He couldn't understand the kids who cried when the bullies called them mean names in order to make their friends laugh. He couldn't see what the big deal was. He couldn't relate to their problems, because his were so different.

If you asked Sam where he was from, he wouldn't be able to tell you. Sam had spent every single year of his life at a different school in a different town with different friends. Sam used to keep track. He used to remember the names of the towns and the names of his friends. He used to keep a scrapbook full of their pictures, but now he just left the pages blank. He couldn't keep up. Before he'd finished creating a collage to help him remember the last town, his parents were making plans to move to the next one. Sam's father was a general in the army. He was a quiet, soft-spoken man who had four children by his lovely wife, Iris. Sam was the youngest, the oldest was 25. Sam didn't know his father very well, but he enjoyed playing games of chess and checkers with him before bedtime, games that didn't require talking. Sam's father never said much to him. He figured that he spent all of his words at work. Sam's older sister, June, started calling Iris by her first name when she was 14 because she was convinced that Iris wasn't her real mother. Iris was nothing like her. Iris was nothing like any of her children, for that matter. She was also unlike most mothers because she didn't seem to mind that her children all started calling her by her first name. Finally, Sam's father decided that it was time to retire, invest some money, and stay put for a while. Sam was quite fond of that idea. He was tired of newness. He was tired of new cities, new houses, and new friends. He was tired of shopping for new decorations with Iris only because Iris hadn't found the new babysitter yet.

And so Sam's family arrived in Lockwood with the intention of staying. Iris enrolled Sam in Lockwood Elementary. He would be starting in the middle of the year, but it didn't matter to Sam. Sam was used to that. It was always harder to make friends when you started in the middle of a school year. It was kind of like showing up to play softball after both sides had already picked their teams.

Sam's first day of school at Lockwood Elementary wasn't much different from his first day at all of the other schools, except for one small detail. Usually Sam sat alone for a few days. Then someone would approach him and attempt to be his friend. Sam couldn't always relate to the kids that approached him. They would ask him a million questions about where he came from and why he arrived at their school in the middle of the year. But sometimes it didn't matter if he liked them or not, Sam just needed someone to eat lunch with so that everyone didn't make fun of him. However, on his first day at Lockwood, Sam only sat alone for a few moments rather than a few days.

Marc sat down across from Sam at one of the empty lunch tables. "I don't have anyone to eat lunch with either," said Marc. He proceeded to unpack his lunch and the two of them ate in silence until Sam broke the silence by asking Marc's name. Sam liked Marc immediately. He knew that Marc had approached him because it was the only logical thing to do. He knew that Marc wouldn't pry into his life like all the other kids did; Sam would have to offer up the information he wanted to share and somehow that made Sam want to share instead of keeping everything locked away. He knew that Marc sat down across from him because two at a table is better than one. Sam immediately took a liking to Marc's no-nonsense attitude. Sam and Marc became instant friends. They understood one another without having to say a word. Marc knew when it was best to keep quiet and not ask Sam what was bothering him. Sam knew when to suggest having Marc come over to his place instead of heading home to an empty house—empty except for Esmerelda doing the household chores. It's not surprising that the two boys became the best of friends. They never agreed on it; it just sort of happened that way. They relied on each other and they knew they always would. It seemed like nothing could ever stand in the way of a friendship so strong. Then junior high school happened.

The first day of junior high school was nerve-wracking for both of them. Sure, they had each other, but they also had a bunch of kids they didn't know to contend with. See, there were three elementary schools that emptied into one junior high school. That meant that two out of every three kids would be unfamiliar to Sam and Marc. It might not sound like that big of a deal, but it was. When you're 12 years old everything feels like a big deal, and change—change feels like the end of the world. It took a while, but eventually Sam and Marc settled into a new way of life. They made other friends, boys that came from different elementary schools. The boys they hung out with most, Kai and Andy, were also best friends, so there was no competition. When three people are all close friends, one person is bound to feel left out. That was never the case with them because Sam had Marc and Kai had Andy, but they also had each other. It seemed perfect, almost too perfect. The four of them weren't popular. They didn't care much for having a ton of friends; having each other was enough. They didn't care much for worrying about what was cool; they liked what they liked for their own reasons. Everyone was content eating lunch under the same tree next to the cafeteria everyday. Well, Sam was almost content eating lunch in the same place day after day.

Sam loved his friends more than anything in the world. He loved the tree they sat under. The only problem was there was this girl, this girl who sat at the other side of the cafeteria at the popular kids' lunch table. Her name was Andrea. She had sandy brown hair and light blue eyes. She was tall and a bit too thin, but she had a beautiful face, a face you had a hard time forgetting. Sam couldn't forget the way she looked at him the day she caught him staring at her. She wasn't surprised, but she was pleased. Sam could tell that the attraction was mutual. That was it though. Sam had all the makings of a popular boy. He was handsome and athletic enough, but Andrea still never approached him. She only stared at him if he stared at her first. Andrea knew that the popular girls were not supposed to be interested in boys that weren't in their crowd. The only way Sam could have a chance with Andrea would be if he found a way to sit with the popular kids at their lunch table. As soon as that thought went through his head he abandoned it. He didn't want to leave Marc and Kai and Andy, and even if he did, it would be virtually impossible to find himself a seat at that table. You couldn't become one of the popular kids just because you decided to be one of them. You had to be invited.

But then Sam received his invitation. It was an invitation to Zack's birthday party. Zack was like the president of the club when it came to the popular kids. He ran the show. If Zack said you were cool, then you were cool. The question is why was Sam chosen to be the next cool kid on the block? The answer was simple: Andrea. Andrea liked Sam and she could tell that Sam liked her. But the only way she would be allowed to like Sam would be if Zack liked Sam first. The only problem was that Zack liked Andrea. He had a crush on Andrea but she never returned his feelings. The second best thing was to become Andrea's closest friend. So that's when the blue card with the tiny yellow balloons appeared on Sam's desk. He opened it up and read it carefully several times. He couldn't understand why Zack wanted him at his birthday party. Maybe Zack was inviting everyone in the entire school, or maybe he was inviting him so that everyone could make fun of him. It didn't make any sense. The first topic during lunch that fateful day was the invitation. Marc seemed to think something was fishy, and Kai and Andy thought it must be a mistake. While the boys were staring at the card in bewilderment Andrea walked by. All four of the boys glanced up, feeling Andrea's eyes on Sam.

"I'll see you at the party, Sam," said Andrea with that careless smile of hers. Sam opened his mouth to speak, but the words weren't there, so he forced a smile as his cheeks flushed bright red. Sam knew in that instant that he had to attend that party. Marc also knew it, and so did Kai and Andy. The difference was, however, that Sam was ecstatic and Marc, Kai, and Andy weren't so sure that it was a good idea.

The day of the party arrived. Sam had never been so nervous in all of his life. He was afraid that no one would talk to him and that everyone would laugh at him. Of course Marc encouraged him and told him that that would never happen. Marc was right. Sam was treated like royalty. Zack latched on to him the minute he walked through the door. He gave Sam a seat at his party table, a seat next to Andrea. Sam felt like he was trapped in his own movie, a movie in which everything turns out the way you want it to. Andrea talked to him the whole night. She even asked him to dance. Then when it was time to go home, Zack told Sam that he should come and hang out on Monday with them, *them* being the popular kids. Sam was on cloud nine for the rest of the day until it dawned on him that there might a problem. What would Marc and Kai and Andy have to say about all of this? Would they care if Sam didn't sit with them all the time? Would the popular kids care if he only sat with them for part of the time? What would Andrea think through all of this? Sam didn't even want to think about that.

Monday arrived and Sam was even more nervous than he had been before the party. He sat behind Marc in homeroom. He couldn't think straight anymore. He just had to do something, so he explained his dilemma to Marc. Marc was very understanding even though deep down he was starting to worry. He was afraid that he might lose his best friend to the popular kids. Marc thought about putting up a fight, but he decided it wasn't worth it. If Sam decided to abandon him, there would be nothing he could say to stop him. So when the fourth period bell rang signaling the beginning of lunch, Sam headed toward the cafeteria. Marc headed toward the tree where Kai and Andy were already sitting watching in disbelief as Sam found himself a seat at the popular table. Andy seemed to think that was that. Sam would never be seen with them again. Marc had more faith in Sam. At least he was trying to. Sam, on the other hand, was having a great time. Andrea had asked him to help her with her Spanish homework, and Zack was treating him like he was one of his best friends. Then as lunch came to an end Zack extended an invitation to Sam to come sit with them the next day. Sam said he would try, but that he might have to sit with some of his other friends. As soon as Sam said these words, he knew he shouldn't have.

"You know, Sam, you can't just sit with us whenever you feel like it. You're either with us or you're not, and your other friends are definitely not with us," said Zack casually.

Sam's heart sank. Zack was asking him to choose, but he wanted it all. He wanted to hang out with Zack and the popular kids because he wanted to get to know Andrea, but he also wanted to hang out with Marc and Kai and Andy because they were his true friends. The decision didn't seem all that difficult until Andrea rested her hand on his shoulder and said, "See you after school." It was going to be their first study session together.

On his way to his next class, all Sam could think about was Marc. He couldn't wait to tell Marc about his conversations with Andrea, every single little detail. Sam always needed to talk to Marc when something important happened, whether it was good or bad. Somehow the news about Andrea didn't seem like such great news without Marc to share it with. How could he trade Marc in for Zack? Zack didn't even know Sam. He didn't know what his favorite food was or even what his favorite sport was. He didn't know about all the different places that Sam had lived, and he didn't know that his father didn't speak to him much and that he never really got along with his mother. No, those were the things Marc cared about and that's why Marc was his best friend. Marc understood Sam, and he liked him all the more because he understood him.

It would be hard to let Andrea down, but it would be even harder to let Marc down. Marc was always there for him when he needed him most. Somehow Sam knew everything would be all right because he had Marc on his side. Marc would know how to put the situation with Andrea into proper perspective. And so Sam tutored Andrea in the library that afternoon, while Marc walked home by himself, worried that he was losing his best friend. But Sam flirted with Andrea and smiled shyly knowing that this was probably the last time he would ever have her undivided attention. He couldn't trade in his friends for the popular kids. His friends were too important to him.

Later that afternoon, when Sam got home, the first thing he did was call Marc. Marc was almost surprised to hear his voice on the other end of the line. The first thing Sam said was sorry. He didn't have to say why; Marc understood completely. Marc knew that for a moment Sam had thought about permanently leaving behind his place under the tree in order to be accepted at the popular table. Marc knew that Sam had come to his senses and realized what he had to gain wasn't worth what he would have to give up. At school the next day, Zack was mortified. How dare Sam turn down his invitation to be one of them? Andrea was disappointed. She wasn't confident enough to let herself like Sam if he wasn't part of the right crowd. Marc and Sam and Kai and Andy—well, they just laughed about it all because they had each other, and the popular kids only had their reputation. Of course Sam and Marc's friendship became stronger than ever. It was stronger because it survived its first test and both of them knew it would survive any test to come.

Reading Guide: "The Friendship Test"

Sam and Marc discover what real friendship means and, yes, that it can defeat popularity, as they are faced with choices of belonging to cliques or remaining loyal to friends.

Messages

Friends share a special bond that is hard to break.
Friendship means accepting others for who they are.
Friends respect their differences.
The ultimate test of friendship is always being there for each
    other.
Friends don't make you choose between themselves and others.
Popularity is never a substitute for friendship.
Friendship is about understanding and caring.

Children Learn

A friend is someone who:
    You want to talk to about anything
    Is understanding and cares
    Shares
    Is loyal and stands up for you
    You can depend on in good times and bad

Questions for Discussion

1. How and why did Sam and Marc become friends?
2. How were they different? How did they deal with their differences?
3. What are your friends like? Are they like you or very different?
4. Is popularity important to the boys? To you?
5. What choice was Zack asking Sam to make?
6. What choice did he ultimately make?
7. Do real friends ask you to choose?
8. Could you have traded a friend like Marc for Zack? Why? Why not?
9. If you had been in Sam's shoes, what would you have done?
10. Was Marc afraid he would lose his friend? How did he handle it? What would you have done?
11. Why did Sam apologize to Marc?
12. "Marc, Sam, Kai, and Andy laughed about it because they had each other and the popular kids only had their reputation." What does this mean? Do you agree? Why?
13. Why was Zack "mortified" by Sam's choice?
14. What was the friendship test? Would you have passed it? Explain.

JULIE LONELY

Julie was the kind of girl who could befriend anyone. She was kind and charming; she was patient and witty. Julie, however, didn't have any friends. She found herself lonely and disconnected from the other kids at school. She usually ate lunch by herself. Sometimes she sat in the library staring at the words on a page without seeing them just to avoid the humiliation of sitting alone in a junior high school cafeteria. Sometimes the other kids made fun of her for always being alone.

Julie lived out little fantasies in her head in order to pass the time. She envisioned kids coming up to her and asking her to sit with them at their lunch tables. She dreamed of being chosen first when it was time to pick teams in gym class. She imagined the cutest boy in school dying to take her in his arms at one of the junior high school dances. These dreams were all Julie really had because reality seemed so far away for her. She didn't have even one friend. Julie never stopped to ask herself why. She just accepted loneliness as her fate. She never attempted to make friends, and she had forgotten why she stopped trying.

* * *

"Julie! Lana's here," called Julie's mom from the kitchen. Julie flew down the stairs at top speed, practically tripping over the toys her little brother, Billy, had left strewn all over the floor. Lana was Julie's best friend. The girls had been best friends since they could hardly walk. They were practically inseparable. Every day after kindergarten they went to each other's houses for snacks and naptime. When it started getting late and it was time for one of the girls to go home, tears were usually shed.

On a slightly overcast day, the girls were particularly excited to see each other. Lana had been away for about a week now and they had a lot of catching up to do. Julie took Lana by the hand and whisked her off to the playroom. A new doll awaited them, one with ruffled dresses and tiny pink bows in her hair. Lana loved Julie's playroom almost as much as she loved Julie herself. It had high ceilings and wall-to-wall toys—Barbies, teddy bears, board games, a play kitchen, and a Victorian-style dollhouse. Julie had all the toys that some little girls only dream of. Lana was one of those little girls. Lana didn't have a playroom at her house. In fact she didn't even have her own bedroom. She shared a room with her little brother, Danny. The two of them also shared toys—teddy bears that were missing an arm or an eye and board games that were missing all the important pieces.

Julie enjoyed sharing her toys with Lana because she enjoyed Lana's company more than all of her favorite toys combined. Without Lana around to share everything with, her dolls' eyes somehow looked sad, and her play kitchen suddenly looked fake. The toys seemed boring to Julie until Lana brought them to life. Lana, on the other hand, never saw the playroom in the boring light that Julie observed. She wanted a playroom of her own. As the girls admired the bright green eyes and heart-shaped lips of Julie's new doll, a conversation took place downstairs that neither of them could hear.

"I'd prefer it if the girls didn't see each other anymore," stated Lana's mother blankly. Julie's mother was taken completely by surprise. She neither expected nor understood what was being said. "Lana comes home from your house wishing it was hers. She demands the same toys Julie has and with her father out of work we can't afford to compete. I think it would be best if Lana spent less time here and more time at home."

"Tearing the girls away from each other doesn't seem like a solution, maybe if we could all just sit down and talk about it—"

"We've made our decision," said Lana's mother abruptly. The conversation was obviously closed. Nothing Julie's mother could say would change her mind. "Lana! It's time to go."

The girls came spilling into the kitchen laughing. The tension on their mothers' faces suffocated their laughter instantly. They looked at one another knowing that something was wrong, very wrong. "Say goodbye, Lana."

Tears and confusion followed. How do you go about explaining to a five-year-old that she can't see her best friend anymore because she has too many toys? Well, Julie would have given up all of her toys if she had been given the choice. It wasn't that simple, though. That day, as Julie's mother explained to her that Lana wouldn't be coming over anymore, something inside Julie broke. It was like she had lost something that could never be replaced. She couldn't understand how or why she had lost it, but somehow she knew it was gone.

* * *

And so Julie sat alone in the library leafing through a magazine not because she couldn't have friends, but because a part of her didn't want them. She never made the effort, thinking that if you don't have something, you can't lose it. Julie never again wanted to feel the way she felt the day Lana disappeared from her life forever. She figured that the best way to avoid that feeling was to maintain her distance from everyone and calmly ignore the kids that made fun of her for maintaining such a distance. Julie probably would have continued along at the same even pace, if Melody hadn't arrived at school.

Melody moved around a lot. Her mother's job took her family from one school to another, sometimes more than twice a year. Melody had no problem making friends. She told you everything there was to know about her calmly and quickly. For Melody there was no time to waste, for she never knew when her mother would insist that it was time to move again. Melody's first day at Mercer Junior High School was eventful, as were most of her first days at new schools. She found most of the girls to be snobby and unresponsive to her outgoing tendencies. But then there was this one girl who sat by herself looking lonely, looking almost comfortable in her loneliness. The other kids made fun of her for it, but Melody didn't care. She was intrigued by her. At first the girl appeared frightened, like a deer caught in headlights. She kept glancing down at the book she was reading like she was hoping the words on the page would interrupt their conversation. Melody was smart for her age. She knew that the girl was giving off all the signs that read, "I really don't want to talk to you." But something also told Melody that this girl wanted to talk more than anyone she'd met in a long time.

Melody eventually pried out of her the essential facts: where she was from, how long she had been at this school, and her name—Julie. The question-and-answer conversation with Julie was grueling, so Melody tried something else. She just kept talking, offering up information about her own life, hoping to make Julie more comfortable. It worked. Eventually the words started spilling out of Julie's mouth. She had so much to say that she felt the need to speak fast for fear she might run out of time. Melody enjoyed every moment of their conversation for she could tell Julie wasn't the kind of girl who opened up easily to people. It seemed like the beginning of a beautiful friendship. Unfortunately, it's not that easy to overcome your fears. They creep up on you when you least expect them.

Sometimes they intervene even when you've decided you have no use for them.

See, Julie and Melody started off strong. Melody was in the driver's seat. She took command of the friendship and managed to pull Julie out of her shell. Julie was happier than she had been in a long time. She liked the fact that Melody made everything easier for her. When she was timid, Melody did the talking. When she was insecure about calling to make plans, Melody was the one who picked up the phone. If the other kids made fun of her, Melody was the one who stood up to them. The girls became close quickly. Pretty soon they were eating lunch together every day at school, studying for tests with one another, and sleeping over at each other's houses on weekends. Everything was perfect from Julie's perspective. Their friendship made Julie feel good about herself in a way she hadn't felt in a while. Melody, on the other hand, began to suffer doubt. Did Julie care to be her friend, or was it just that she didn't have anyone else? Was it just that Melody made friendship easy for her? Of course Melody didn't think about things in terms of these exact questions. She didn't quite know how to put her feelings about the situation into words. She just knew that she felt unsettled, like something wasn't quite right. And that's why she didn't call. All of sudden she was tired of always having to initiate everything. Let Julie call her and suggest plans for the weekend. Let Julie suggest a good time for them to study together.

Melody just wanted Julie to make an effort. To have a friend you have to be a friend. Well, unfortunately, when Julie was called on to be a friend, her fear reared its ugly head. When her phone didn't ring for the next few days, it didn't occur to her to pick up the phone and call Melody. No, she assumed the worst: that their friendship was over for some unimaginable reason. And so Julie began avoiding Melody. She spent lunch in the library. She passed through the halls with her head held down. During class she stared at either the teacher or her desk intently just in case Melody decided to try and establish eye contact.

At first Julie thought she could go on like this forever. She had done it before, so why not now? Well, the problem was that Julie finally realized that she was a wimp. She realized she had walked away from things that turned her stomach upside down. She realized she was afraid of having friends, but she also felt like she didn't have the strength to do anything about it. Julie was hurting. She was hurting because she was losing Melody as a friend, someone who had become important to her. She didn't want to eat her lunch alone to sounds of kids snickering behind her back. She hated herself for not picking up the phone and calling Melody even though part of her was well aware that Melody was waiting to hear from her. Everything stayed the same for several days.

Then one gloomy afternoon something changed. Sixth-period English was just about over, which meant school was just about to let out. Mrs. Miller was assigning each student a poem to interpret. It was homework, weekend homework, which of course drew many sighs of disgust from her pupils. Julie didn't mind. She had nothing else to do over the weekend. The bell sounded. "As soon as I assign you a page number, you're free to leave," said Mrs. Miller. The kids who had their assignments darted for the door.

"Julie Pallone. Chapter 1, page 22." Julie wrote down the numbers and packed up her books carefully. She was in no hurry get anywhere for there was nowhere she really felt like being.

Julie decided to do her homework as soon as she got home. No sense in sitting around thinking about how boring her weekend was going to be. English was her first choice. She was good at math even though she found it incredibly dull. Poetry, novels, and short stories—the way an author arranged words on paper—that's what Julie enjoyed most. So she opened her literature book to chapter 1, page 22, looking for her assignment.

Lonely are those who do not know the meaning of two.
Lonely are those who fear two must always end in one.
Lonely are those who feel without speaking.
Lonely are those who walk through life without waking.
A.R.

Julie sat at the kitchen table for an extended period of time, staring absently at the page that held these four lines. Her after-school snack, a bowl of chocolate chip ice cream, sat melting beside her.

Page 22. She thought. Yes, it was the right page. Had Mrs. Miller assigned her this poem purposely? No, it was just a coincidence. Right? Julie read the poem over and over again, muttering the words under her breath. It wasn't one of those poems that had strange sentence structure or words you sometimes can't even find in the dictionary. It was simple and straightforward. It said so much without saying a lot. Julie rested her head in her hands and tried to decide which one of those lines explained her loneliness. A wave of emptiness washed over her when she came to realize that every one of them did. She picked up the phone and dialed Melody's number.

Reading Guide: "Julie Lonely"

Julie learns the real meaning of friendship and that "To have a friend, you must be a friend."

Messages

> Life is lonely without friends.
> Friendship is a two-way street. It means giving and taking.
> One needs to face problems, not run from them.
> We are social creatures and need friends.

Children Learn

> To have a friend, you must be a friend.
> You have to work at friendship for it to grow.
> Each friend must take the initiative in the relationship to contribute.
> Friendship is about sharing, caring, and being there for the other.

Questions for Discussion

> 1. In the beginning did Julie want friends?
> 2. Why didn't Julie want to try and make friends? Was it a good reason? How would you have acted in the same situation?

3. Why didn't Lana's mom want the girls to continue their friendship?
4. Do you think that she was being fair? How else could she have handled it?
5. How did Julie and Lana feel about their friendship ending? How did they react?
6. How would you feel if you lost your best friend?
7. How did Julie change when she met Melody?
8. How would you describe their friendship in the beginning? Was it a two-way street?
9. Why was Melody feeling doubtful about their friendship?
10. How did Julie interpret the poem?
11. How did it change their friendship in the end?

15

DEALING WITH
THE BULLY

Charles, a five-year-old, would constantly get into fights at preschool. He acted like a little dictator, telling everyone what to do, taking toys from others if he wanted them, and using physical means such as hitting and kicking to get his way. His favorite victim was John, who would just cry. The principal called the parents in for a conference after efforts at school didn't seem to work.

A STEP-BY-STEP SUCCESS STORY

The parents decided that they had to accept this behavior as really serious behavior that had to stop. It was important to support each other—the school and the parents—in their quest to change this behavior. A plan was designed to deal with Charles's behavior both at home and in school. The essence of the plan was to remove Charles from activities when he misbehaved. Clear and firm limits against unacceptable behavior were established and communicated in school and at home. Lastly, nonphysical and nonhostile consequences were consistently applied when the rules were broken. Praise was given generously to reinforce appropriate behaviors.

The parents took the following steps at home:

1. When Charles became aggressive with peers (bossing them around, yelling, or hitting them) he would immediately be removed from the situation. He was taken to a time-out room. As the parent took Charles to the time-out room, Charles was told in a calm and firm tone of voice that he couldn't play with if he was going to fight. Nothing more was said.

2. A timer in the time-out room was set for three minutes. If Charles did not cooperate, another minute would be added to the time. Yelling and tantrum time was not counted. After the time-out was over, he was allowed to return to the activities with no further comments made.

3. The parents observed all play and interactions that Charles had with others. When they saw Charles interacting in a cooperative manner for at least five minutes they would praise the behavior or serve treats to reinforce it. They made comments like: "I really like the way you are sharing the crayons," or "You are playing very nicely together."

Certain minor aggressive acts and acts the parents learned about later were ignored if not serious. They didn't want to overdo the time-out program and they wanted the association of the behavior with the consequence closely connected to be most effective. The key here was that this process was followed consistently to address Charles's aggressive and bully behavior when caught in the act, so that the penalty was more meaningful and clearly associated with the act.

If you think this sounds a little bit like the old "Pavlov's conditioning," you're right. Just as Pavlov was training dogs to salivate at the sound of a bell by conditioning them to associate the bell with food, so too were the parents training Charles to associate unacceptable behaviors with time-out and leaving fun play. Eventually, the hope was that Charles would think before he acted and realize that hitting would only get him a negative consequence—a time-out; while peaceful cooperative behavior would lead to positive consequences. Such a program of rewards and penalties consistently followed can quickly have tremendous results. Keep in mind that any deviation, even once or twice from this routine, may sabotage efforts to change the behavior.

THE STEPS

It's not easy to face the fact that your child may be acting like a bully. When parents are confronted with this label, the most attractive response is one of denial. Making excuses for the behavior and playing it down follow closely in second and third place as reactions to the news. "No, not Jack. That's ridiculous!" "Everyone does this . . . he doesn't mean it maliciously." "He doesn't even understand the meaning of his words."

Hard to believe parents would say these things? They do. These are very common responses from parents, and why not? Parents often will view the bully label as an attack not only against their child but also against their child-rearing practices. It's hard not to take it personally. Depending on the age of the child, there are definite steps parents and the school can do to reverse this situation. Working together, as in Charles's case, is the key. The earlier it's done, the better. The sooner it is dealt with, the less likely the bully behavior will become a habitual part of an aggressive personality. Being proactive in raising children (as described in chapters 19–21) is clearly the best approach to prevent the problem before it happens. Creating an environment where bullying just cannot survive means there is no issue to deal with later. But when a situation arises, there are some techniques to reverse the situation.

SEARCH FOR REASONS

Once you have accepted the fact that your child is a bully or at a minimum engages in bully behaviors, the next step is to search for reasons why. Start asking yourself questions: Is the child a pure bully or bully/victim? Is he acting from a base of anger or desire for power and control? Is my child imitating my behavior? Have I not demonstrated or taught my child the appropriate social skills to relate to others? Does he know how to deal with conflict? Have I been loving and affectionate? Am I too permissive? Am I too critical? Do I give enough praise for the positive behaviors? Have I set clear limits and followed through enforcing them? Finding out the reasons behind this behavior can be the key to remedying the situation. Once you know why, you can find techniques and approaches that could reverse the situation. Unfortunately, answering the question why may not always be as easy as it sounds. But it certainly is a place to start.

ANTIBULLY STRATEGIES AND TECHNIQUES

Expose Your Child to Positive Role Models

Positive role models, whether parents, teachers, or other important adults in children's lives, can make quite an impact on growing children. If children are engaging in bully behavior, parents need to examine their own behavior. Parents should reduce any hostile, aggressive behavior they engage in, especially in the home. If children are imitating aggressive or angry behaviors that they live with at home, it's time for parents to make some changes. If parents hit each other, throw things, or scream at each other, the children may very well incorporate these actions into their own behavior. Children who receive harsh, physical punishment at the hands of parents may go out and inflict this cruelty on others.

Moreover, a number of research studies have concluded further that children who view aggressive acts by others on television tend to act more aggressively themselves—thus the movement to restrict children's exposure to violence on television, in films, and video games. A recent study at the University of Washington in Seattle concluded that the more television four-year-olds watch, the more likely they are to be mean and cruel to others by the time they reach age eleven. The study suggests that this is because the escalating amount of violent content on television, especially in cartoons, is increasingly accepted and imitated by children.

Setting Limits in the Home

When parents engage in firm and fair discipline, children grow up to be fair and responsible themselves. Being firm means setting fair rules, communicating them, and then enforcing them in a peaceful and non-violent manner. It means letting children know that teasing and other bully behaviors are not allowed and will not be tolerated. Parents are the key in terms of guiding the children's behavior. Parents need to take control and set limits for behavior starting when their children are very young. When they don't, children keep testing to find those limits and we see out-of-control kids who very well may exhibit bully behaviors. Children want to know where their limits are: what is allowed and what is not. Then there is no need to constantly test to find out. When children understand where they are, they feel more comfortable. They know what to expect. Their world is not as stressful.

How do we set limits? How do we guide our children so they act responsibly? One way is to use the approach that Charles's parents followed. Focusing attention on the positive and ignoring the negative behavior can be a very successful approach to extinguishing unacceptable behaviors. Let's take a closer look. Our response to children's behavior sends a message of approval or disapproval. All children inherently want approval from the most important people in their world, their parents. We know that when we reward (praise) a behavior, it is usually repeated again, because children want to please us. On the other hand, when we ignore behaviors, there is no incentive to repeat it. Watch out. Too often adults take positive behaviors for granted and fail to praise them because it is expected. But if we praise good behavior it will be repeated. For example: When your child, let's say age three, plays well with a friend and exhibits cooperative behavior, praise him. "Jack I like how you and Tanner are sharing your toys. Great job!" Note, your praise should be specific and describe behaviors you want to reward. To say to Jack, "You're a good boy today," gives him no feedback. Where aggressive behavior has been an issue, you might want to give praise every 5 to 10 minutes. "That's great how you guys aren't fighting" or " I like the way you took turns playing with the truck."

Parents need to understand that young children respond to the special attention you give them when you praise them. This is why you don't want to give any special attention when they do something wrong. I have seen too many children rewarded when they are able to "push their parents' buttons." Here's a good example: Little Danny loved to come to my house. We had this large pool in the backyard with a row of stones around its perimeter. Danny, age three at the time, loved to throw the stones into the pool, to our dismay. Danny's Dad would yell at him to stop, but the more Dad yelled, the more stones went into the pool. A similar case is the first grader who constantly seeks the attention of the teacher by misbehaving. Often any kind of attention, negative or positive, can reinforce behaviors. We don't want to spend too much time giving excessive negative attention to behaviors we are trying to eliminate.

What we want to do is ignore a child's poor behavior as long as it doesn't pose a danger to anyone. For example: Jack is acting very aggressively in play toward Tanner and grabs a toy from him because he wants to play with it. Focus your attention on Tanner, who is being victimized, showing concern and empathy for him. As for Jack, very calmly and with a firm voice tell him, "Taking someone's toy is not okay." Then quickly return your attention to Tanner. A time-out often works well in this situation, because the child is being removed from the fun and play and basically is being ignored.

The key then is to find a balance. Reward children with praise, treats, and so forth, every time you can catch them being good. Ignore as many of the negative acts as possible, so that attention is focused only on good behavior and the child isn't being rewarded with attention through your nagging, scolding, or punishing. When necessary, use the time-out for unprovoked aggression. Do this with as little interaction and dialogue with your child as possible. Remember we don't want to pay a lot of attention to negative behavior but simply remove the child from the situation. When one child is bullying another, focus attention and compassion on the victim of the bully behaviors. Shower the injured party with nurturance, concern, and compassion. Be a model of empathy for the child and again send the message that bully behavior does not get attention.

Using Time-Out to Deal With Bully-Type Behavior

Time-out is an effective strategy to send a clear message to children that certain behaviors are unacceptable. It helps to set clear boundaries and limits for their behavior. When this strategy is consistently followed, children learn quickly that unprovoked aggressive acts will not be allowed.

A time-out is a particular period of time in which children are removed and isolated from some activity and taken to another area of the house or classroom. The length of the timeout should depend on the age of the child. For example, three-to-five-year-olds might be given a two-minute time-out when they demonstrate rude or bully-type behavior. The children are brought to a predetermined room (a room without toys, computer, television, or anything with which to entertain themselves) with a simple and brief explanation ("You hit Ashley. You cannot play and hit others."). A timer is set, and the children are told that they may return when the timer rings. During the two minutes there should be no talking or interaction with the children. If children are uncooperative and refuse to stay in the room or have a tantrum, increase the time-out by another minute. It may be necessary to do this a few times and again explain briefly that when they stay in the room and cooperate they can come out.

When the time-out is over and children return to their activities, look for opportunities to send praise when their behavior calls for it. This is very important. We want to do away with the uncooperative behaviors but at the same time look for and reinforce desirable substitute behaviors. Saying things like, "That was great that you waited your turn to use the truck after Jason," reinforces behaviors of sharing and patience. For older, school-age children, start with 5- to 10-minute time-outs and increase with additional 5-minute intervals if there is a lack of cooperation.

TEACHING YOUR CHILD IMPORTANT SOCIAL SKILLS

Children often will become aggressive toward others simply because they do not have the necessary social skills or empathy to act appropriately in certain situations. Somewhere along the way they haven't been taught, or just haven't learned for one reason or another, the important social skills of how to be a friend and what that means. They haven't learned to be assertive rather than aggressive, or to use their words instead of their hands to deal with conflict. Anger gets the best of them. We need to help children deal with and express all their feelings, especially anger, if this is a problem. Alternative and acceptable ways to express anger can be provided through play activities. This provides children with an opportunity to release anger without directing it toward others. Sports such as football provide children an outlet to release angry feelings, eliminating the need to act hostilely toward others. Teaching anger management, friendship, and conflict resolution skills is outlined in chapter 20 and 21.

Fostering empathy in children is another important approach. Often bullies are lacking in their ability to be empathetic. They don't seem to understand the impact of their actions on others' feelings. How it feels to be in another's shoes is a hard concept for some children to get. As far as they are concerned, their victims have no feelings. This allows them to hurt others with their words or hands with little or no conscience. The more children have compassion and concern for others, the less likely they are to hurt them. We can teach children to be empathetic by modeling it ourselves as adults and using all opportunities to point out how others feel when "bad" things happen to them. When children try to hit or kick another, explain to them that it "hurts" the other person. Ask them, "How would you feel if Jason kicked you like that?"

16

TAKING AWAY SUPPORT FOR THE BULLY

An Effective School Program

The goal of any effective school program is to take away *all* support for the bully. Bullying has been able to flourish in schools today because too often the school community is unknowingly supporting the bully. When adults treat bullying with an attitude that says "no big deal—we've all been teased—nothing new," they support the bully. When adults and kids on a campus look the other way when bullying occurs, they support the bully. When students act as participants or even bystanders and do nothing, they support the bully. When a school fails to supervise a campus properly, it supports the bully. When parents get defensive and refuse to accept responsibility for children's behavioral problems, they support the bully. When a school does not have a program that addresses bullying, it supports the bully.

If model programs successfully used in schools today are examined, common elements can be found. The programs:

Involve all stakeholders: school staff, parents, and community
Raise the level of awareness of all stakeholders on the issue of bullying
Mobilize the entire school and community to commit to changing its culture
Expect all to support the victim and confront the bully
Include ongoing education for all stakeholders

Set clear rules and consequences
Provide proper supervision to monitor the campus

Communication is step one. The issue of bullying must be brought into the open and talked about. The whole community should be made aware that at this school there is or will be an antibully program. A zero-tolerance approach to bullying is advertised over and over and over again. Just taking this issue to the forefront and no longer "burying our heads in the sand" will start to make everyone feel safe, so that learning can occur. Parents must not be afraid to ask their children or the school the important questions.

Such an antibully program begins with an assessment of the problem. Students fill out an anonymous survey to measure the degree to which bullying is a problem on the school campus. After all, it is the students who know about bullying. The results of the survey should be published and discussed openly with the entire community, so that an action plan can be designed that sets clear expectations and goals for the program.

Ongoing training programs should be set up for staff and parents to develop an understanding and consensus on what bullying is all about, how to spot it, how to intervene, and how to encourage children to open up and feel safe talking to an adult. Teachers and parents need to be taught how to deal with bullying situations without becoming the judge and jury. They need to model and teach problem solving and conflict resolution.

A strong supervision program must be designed so no area of the campus is available to the bully. Every adult on campus is expected to be vigilant, to be on the lookout for red flags, and to intervene when necessary. Campus supervisors are put through training before they work on the campus.

A clear set of rules and progressive consequences is communicated to all. Progressive consequences should match the infraction. The consequences escalate depending on the seriousness of the behavior and whether it is a first, second, or often-repeated offense. Consequences may range from a lunchtime detention to suspension to expulsion. Rules and consequences are communicated to all students and parents. Consequences are enforced consistently. This is important, because ineffective enforcement may make the problem worse.

An ongoing curriculum for all students focuses on antibullying and character education. Assembly programs and classroom lessons are designed to:

1. Educate children about bullying, how to handle it, and their role in preventing it. The goal here is to arm our children, build peer pressure against bullying, and increase support for the victims.
2. Promote peaceful and positive behaviors and reward students who exhibit them.
3. Provide character education, including lessons on kindness, respect, and responsibility.
4. Mobilize all students to commit to and participate in the antibully program.

Support for victims involves teaching children what bullying is all about and how to defeat bullies. Student groups should be set up where students safely and anonymously talk about their experiences. There is an opportunity for them to learn and practice coping skills. Social skills are taught so that victims and all students develop friendship skills and learn to interact with assertiveness and confidence.

Support for the bully means making counseling services available at the school. Discovering why the child engages in the bully behavior is important in determining an approach. Working on anger management, conflict resolution, and building empathy skills is part of an effective program to support the bully. The administrator should have a serious talk with the bully and let him and his parents know that these behaviors will not be tolerated. The bully should work together in small groups with older kids on cooperative projects. Reinforce the child each time he demonstrates caring and prosocial behavior so he sees he can get attention from doing positive things. Work with families to help change the behavior.

Research shows that bullying can be prevented when we act proactively. According to one research brief by Fight Crime: Invest in Kids (an anticrime group of law enforcement officials and victims of violence), "proven programs can cut bullying in half and sharply reduce crime." The brief points to three model programs that have been tested in schools and significantly reduced bullying by including features described above:

The Olweus Bullying Prevention Program
Linking the Interests of Families and Teachers (LIFT)
The Incredible Years

Taking away support of the bully should be at the heart of any antibullying program. Only an effective school program that invites *all* to take part and commit to eradicating bullying behavior will help bully-proof our children.

17

COPING STRATEGIES
FOR VICTIMS

"Nobody can make you feel inferior without your consent."

—Eleanor Roosevelt

Preparation for defeating bullies begins long before children even face a bully. Raising children to be independent, resilient, and strong problem solvers is preparation. These are children with high self-esteem who are able to view themselves not as perfect, but as people who are flawed; who can accept criticism, be teased, and made fun of. These are children that aren't easily upset or don't overreact because others call them names or criticize them.

All adults and caretakers need to support children so they can be free from bullying. This means teaching them how to live happily and productively in the *real world*, not a fairy-tale world where everyone must be nice to each other. Though we can and should strive to make the world a better and kinder place, we cannot raise children to expect it. Children need to learn how to deal with all kinds of people, including bullies. They need to know how to defeat the bullies at their own game. Life is not always fair. There are mean people out there. And if children are not taught how to deal with them, we do them a disservice. In effect we send them out into a jungle ill equipped to meet success.

When bullying is an issue, children need to be made a part of the solution. Children have to be able to solve problems. They learn to only when they are allowed to. In this sense, bullying is *their* problem to face. Parents shouldn't face it for them, no matter how much they would like to. This doesn't mean that parents don't give them guidance, because they should. However, when parents continually shelter children from adversity the message sent is, "You can't, or don't have to, take responsibility for your problems. I'll solve them for you." Later, as adults, these children often blame others for their feelings and problems. Children's self-confidence grows when they solve problems on their own, not when an adult does it for them. It's the old adage: If we give a fish to a poor starving family, we relieve their hunger for a day. When we teach them how to fish, we give them a lifetime of being hunger-free. Solving children's problems for them today only solves that problem today; teaching children problem solving will help them solve their problems for a lifetime.

START TO EDUCATE IN THE HOME AND CONTINUE IN SCHOOL

Begin in the home and then continue at school to educate children to be resilient and tolerant. Prepare them to defeat bullies, by supporting them and equipping them with coping strategies should they be targeted. In short, this means raising and educating kids to refuse to be victims.

The best armor parents and teachers can outfit children with is to feel good about themselves. The sense of power that they feel when they feel good about themselves allows them to see any situation not from the viewpoint of a victim but from the vantage of someone who is proud and doesn't have to get caught up in the bullies' words or what they think. What the bullies say isn't as important as their own opinion of themselves. They know that, "Nobody can make [them] feel inferior without [their] consent." And they're not giving it.

How does the parent or teacher contribute toward raising children with such high self-esteem? Create a positive and loving environment as described in chapter 19. On a daily basis build children's self-esteem with hugs and deserving praise. Remember that criticism and putting children down especially by parents only has the effect of lowering children's self-esteem with the result that they accept themselves as victims and believe the words of bullies. Help children feel good about themselves by taking the time to help them make friends. Friendships help to raise self-esteem. Also, remember it is often the loner child that becomes a victim.

TEACH CHILDREN BY EXAMPLE NOT TO ACT LIKE VICTIMS

Children will imitate parents regardless of what they say or how they tell them to act. If parents are overly sensitive, cannot tolerate criticism, and are easily angered at the slightest insult, offspring too will take themselves way too seriously and easily allow others to upset them, putting themselves constantly into the role of victim. On the other hand, if parents can laugh at themselves and not be hurt by comments from others, children will inherit this resilience.

TEACH CHILDREN "STICK AND STONES"

Teach children that "sticks and stones will break our bones but names will never hurt us." Children need to hear and understand this slogan, see it modeled, and be given practice to live by it. Too often adults, by their actions, teach children inadvertently to react to mean words. If adults don't treat words as so hurtful, then children won't either. Adults sometime send the wrong message, "Oh poor, Jennifer." Jack is so mean to her and is punished because he called her a name. Adults side with the victims and blame the bullies. This teaches children to get upset by words and react to them, thereby promoting bullying and teasing.

Instead adults should be demonstrating for children that "sticks and stones may break your bones, but names will never hurt you." Parents' and teachers' responses to children when they complain about being called names will be an important determinant of children's attitudes and consequently their reactions toward mean words. When adults treat name calling as not such a big deal, so will the kids. If adults don't start to judge who is right or wrong or punish, then children will get the message that name-calling isn't so hurtful. They learn that there is no need to react to it; adults don't. Here is a quick easy response parents and teachers can use in the home between siblings and in the classroom between students to send their message about mean words:

JOHNNY: Jessica called me an idiot!

TEACHER: Is it true?

JOHNNY: No.

TEACHER: Good!

Children learn quickly: What's the big deal? The potential victim learns there is no reason to be upset. When Johnny is praised, the message is Johnny did well by not believing it to be true.

Playing the game "Sticks and Stones Challenge" is a great way to teach children how *not* to react to name-calling and teasing. It demonstrates that bullying is a game with two players: a winner and a loser. The loser becomes the victim. The rules of the game are simple. Two people play. Each person takes turns insulting the other (No curse words are allowed). Each time one player gets angry he/she scores a point. The winner is the person with the least amount of points. The loser is the person with the most points (or the one who gets upset the most). Put a short time limit (15 to 30 seconds) on each round and then reverse roles. It can get very loud, so be careful where this is done and who is within earshot.

TEACH CHILDREN ABOUT FREEDOM OF SPEECH

Teaching children the meaning of freedom of speech is a great place to start, especially with older children. Freedom of speech is actually the constitutional version of the "sticks and stones" slogan. Teach children that laws are set up to punish people who actually hurt others. Teasing words and name-calling that *may* hurt feelings are not prohibited under the Constitution. The reason is because a person's reaction to such words is so subjective. Punishment can't be given because one person may be more sensitive then another. While one person may simply laugh when called an idiot, another could be in tears. Children need to understand that they have to let people say what they want, even if they don't like it sometimes, so that they can say what they want to as well.

TEACH CHILDREN TO BE MORAL INDIVIDUALS

When children learn to live morally, they learn the most important principle of all: tolerance for others. Being tolerant of others, including the intolerant, begets tolerance and may turn enemies into friends. The best way to teach morality is by acting morally. Children will follow the lead. Ask important moral questions to discover whether you are a model for children: Am I treating others the way I want to be treated or treating them the way they treat me? Am I able to "turn the other cheek" or do I seek revenge? Am I judgmental or critical of others?

TEACH CHILDREN NOT TO BE VICTIMS

> *"He who has so little knowledge of human nature as to seek happiness by changing anything but his disposition will waste his life in fruitless efforts."*
>
> —Samuel Johnson

Why do some children get picked on only once, while others are tormented over and over again? Why do some children's feelings get hurt when they are teased or called a name, while others walk around unscathed? Why is it that some children allow comments to "roll off" their backs, while others react so strongly? The simple answer may be that some children make themselves victims unknowingly. They embrace a victim mentality that automatically puts them at the mercy of another. The balance of power shifts when they make themselves victims. The bullies hold the strings, and the victims are their puppets. Can bullies make us angry? Can they make victims seek revenge? Actually the victims are doing it to themselves by acting like victims. Everyone wants to be the winner, not the loser, in a conflict. It is the reward of winning, that power, that brings the bully back to the same victim, or loser, over and over again.

A victim mentality makes anyone powerless to handle bullies. The victim mentality is embraced when children think like victims—thinking that life should be fair and no one has a right to be mean to them. They expect always to be treated well. When bullies attack, they can blame bullies and don't have to take responsibility for the problem or for fixing it because they didn't create it. Someone else should fix it. They get angry and seek revenge. Whenever we get angry at someone we usually feel like a victim. Once we act on the anger or try to get revenge we become a victim. Enter the ever-growing group of bully/victims, who have sought revenge by bullying others. They would have never become bullies had they never become victims.

Children need to learn early on not to embrace this victim mentality. They need to be taught not to react to teasing or bullying, because that's exactly what bullies are looking for. They want to "push buttons." They want anger. Reactions to teasing and bullying will only bring bullies back again and again and make children victims. Here are three basic rules children must learn so they don't become victims:

Don't give another the power to make you angry or upset.
Don't give another power by feeling you must defend yourself.
Don't give another power by attacking back.

When children react by getting angry or upset and feel like they have to defend themselves or attack back to get revenge they make themselves victims. Trying to *stop* bullies by these methods only worsens the situation by ensuring that the bullies have targets they enjoy making fun of.

WHAT IF THE CHILD FALLS INTO THE BULLY'S TRAP?

Your child is showing all the signs of being a victim of bullying or teasing. Immediately open the communication channels as discussed in chapter 13. Before the situation can be remedied, it's important to first discover the nature of the problem your child is having and with whom. Is the child being picked on? Teased? Is he a willing or provocative victim? Is there a pure bully or a bully/victim involved? These are the important questions that need to be asked. How is the child handling it—by acting aggressive or withdrawing?

Always start with listening to the plight of children carefully. Get as much information about the bullying as possible. Be empathetic and supportive, so that children will know you are on their side. Actively listen. If the children are comfortable and give you permission, contact the school and work with them.

Teaching children how to handle bullies must start with an understanding of what bullying is all about. Children need to learn why and how kids bully and what they can do to stop it. Reading stories about bullying can be a great beginning teaching tool. Explain that there are two different kinds of bullies: the pure bully and the bully/victim.

Discuss with children their situation to determine which type of bully is targeting them. If children are just arbitrarily being singled out, a pure bully may be looking for fun by driving them crazy. On the other hand, if children are targeted because the bully is angry or jealous, a bully/victim is seeking revenge. Different strategies may be called for depending on whether it is a pure bully or bully/victim. Sometimes the distinction is not obvious. However, when in doubt, advise children to assume they are dealing with the pure bully and use strategies accordingly.

Give Advice

Start by explaining to victims how they may have fallen into a bully's trap. If bullies are pure bullies, explain that they are simply trying to "push buttons" and get a reaction. It is all about power and control. When children let their buttons get pushed and act really angry or sad or upset, and try to stop it, they have given control to bullies. They can make victims feel that way with their words or actions. They are looking for reactions, which is their reward. The choice is yours. How you respond to someone's mean words or teasing is up to you. Do you want to give them that power? If not, simply don't try to stop them. Don't get angry, don't defend, and don't attack. Don't react. Show them you really don't care.

Coping Strategies

There are a number of strategies to use to defeat bullies. They all basically call for the victims to respond with an "I-don't-care" attitude, and thereby let bullies know that they can keep it up, but they won't get to them and make them victims. Send a clear message: "Keep on coming, I'm not going to try and stop you." Remember, the person who doesn't care, usually has the power. A great book that children will enjoy is *Simon's Hook*, which analogizes the bully to a fisherman and challenges the fish not to take the bait. For children ages five to nine this is a great starting point in developing an understanding of what bullying is about and how to handle it.

Choosing a strategy to deal with bullies is up to the victims. Present all options. The key here is that children should make the choice based on what they are most comfortable doing. Practicing various strategies in role-play can be fun as well. Here are three ways to handle bullying:

Avoid the bullies. It's okay to walk away from mean peers. Ignore their words.

Laugh at the teasing. Humor demonstrates it doesn't bother you. Responding with, "If you think I'm _____, you should see

my mom" is an easy way to use humor to answer an insult. Substitute in the blank: fat, ugly, or any other name you are called.
Agree with the bully. Just mirror back the insult: "You know
you're right, I'm _____."

Teach your child to use positive self-talk when attacked verbally by
another. Here's an opportunity to constantly remind themselves
that this is just a game and that they're going to win.

For some children these strategies may be easier said than done
effectively. Many children will tell you, " I can't help it. He is such a
jerk. He makes me *so* angry and he knows it." The best response
then is, "Okay, so you don't want to win; you want to be the loser."
Here the answer is teaching children anger management and how to
let insults and names "slide off their backs." Both take practice, but
they work when coupled with constant reminders to the victims that
this is how to defeat bullies and win.

Anger management is the prerequisite. Teaching children how to
deal with angry feelings and act cool is so important. Just as children
are taught to compliment each other and be kind to each other
through role-play, they can be taught not to get upset or at least if
they are upset, to control their reaction to insults. See chapter 20 for
a detailed description on dealing with angry feelings. Children need
to learn to be cool and to control their angry feelings when attacked
verbally by another to stop being victimized.

Role-Playing: A Great Teaching Tool

Role-playing is a wonderful opportunity for a parent or teacher or
any adult to demonstrate why some children become targets repeatedly and how to stop it. Do it in a classroom or at home, with a
small group or an individual child.

Step 1: Announce the Rules for the Role-Play

For our purposes we'll use a classroom as the setting, with the role-
play between teacher and student.

1. The student is to tease the teacher, call the teacher names, and put the teacher down. No foul language allowed. Tell the student not to be afraid of hurting the teacher's feelings; in fact that is his goal.
2. The teacher's job is to try and get the student to stop the teasing.
3. There is a winner and a loser here: If the teacher is able to get the student to stop, the teacher wins and the student loses. If the student doesn't stop, the student wins and the teacher loses.

Step 2: Role-Play #1—A Strong Reaction

As the student puts the teacher down repeatedly, the teacher will act increasingly angry and really try to use words, threats, and gestures to try to get the student to stop. It's important to show outwardly your frustration and how upset you are by the comments. Make sure the teacher plays it seriously and does not laugh. The class will probably be laughing up a storm—that's okay. After a while (maybe three or four minutes), when the teacher has had enough, tell the student you give up.

Discussion: What happened? Did I make him stop? Why not? Was there any way I was going to stop him from teasing me if he wanted to? Who won?

Step 3: Role-Play #2—No Reaction

Tell the class that they are going to try this again. The rules are the same. This time however, the teacher will go along with all the teasing and put-downs. Instead of fighting the comments, the teacher accepts them and doesn't get angry. The teacher responds calmly and humorously with phrases like:

"Yeah, you're right."
"I know."
"Everyone says that."

"Oh, well."

"If you think I'm weird, you should see my mom."

The key is to not act arrogantly, but rather show the student that these insults really don't bother you. Here, the teacher keeps going till the student gives up. It may take a bit longer, but probably not much.

Step 4: Guided Discussion

Compare the two scenarios (with expected responses from the class).

What was the difference between the way I acted in the first and second role-play?

I got really angry and overreacted the first time.

The second time I was cool and calm and didn't let it bother me.

Which was more fun for you as the bully?

The first time was much more fun, when you got angry.

The second time it got boring.

Who won each time? Why?

The first time the student won, because the teacher couldn't stop him and gave up.

The second time the teacher won because he got the student to stop.

Who looked stupid each time? Why?

The first time the teacher looked stupid, because she got so angry.

The second time the student looked stupid, because all his teasing didn't bother the teacher.

Who decides how to respond to teasing and bullying? What are my choices?

The teacher could choose to get mad or not to let it bother her.

Which choice is usually more effective and why?

The choice not to act angry but rather act calm and cool as though I was not bothered was the best choice, because there was no longer any reason to continue teasing.

Step 5: Take Comments and Then Summarize

What did you learn about reacting to bullying?

When I reacted angrily and tried to make you stop, I lost. The class even laughed at my behavior because I looked pretty stupid. No way was I going to win. You were having a lot of fun and I was letting you. I was making you continue by making it fun. The only reason it stopped was because I got tired. You probably would have gone all day as long as I kept trying to stop you.

When I did nothing to stop you, you gave up. You looked like the stupid one because you couldn't get a reaction from me. After all when someone calls you names and you don't care, who looks the idiot: you or me? I won. I got you to stop.

Step 6: Test for Understanding

Relate this to a bullying. So what do you think you should do the next time someone calls you the "dork" word? Are you going to try to get him to stop? Why?

The student should basically repeat in his own words your summary.

Step 7: Practice—Reverse the Roles

The teacher now insults the student in the scenario—same rules. If the student appears to be getting upset, stop. Remind him or her that this is just a game and you don't mean what you're saying. You're just trying to help the class learn not to get angry. "If I get you angry, remember, I win." Praise the student when he or she doesn't get angry. "You win. I lose."

Step 8: More Practice

Allow students to practice with each other, first in front of the class and then with partners. Be careful, as this can get pretty noisy. You might want to do this outside. Let them reverse roles and time it, maybe a couple of minutes each role-play. Then review: who was the winner each time and why?

A WARNING: YOU MUST USE IT ALL THE TIME

Once the children demonstrate that in fact they have a clear under-standing of the strategy and how to implement it, they need to be advised how to use it most effectively. Bullies are trying to push but-tons and if they have already succeeded they will be convinced they can do it again. When students don't react initially, the bullies will try harder, figuring that since they got a reaction once, they can do it again. Therefore, for this strategy to work, it must be used 100% of the time. Not 90% or 95% of the time, but all the time from this point forward. Expect the bullying to continue and get worse before bullies give up. But they will give up.

Note that this role-play should be practiced with other strategies in our list. Try role-playing other strategies: ignoring, using humor, walking away—but most importantly with an "I-don't-care" attitude. The teacher should demonstrate, so that body language (standing up tall, eye-to-eye contact, chin up) is modeled correctly for kids.

But What If It Doesn't Work?

Some bullies are relentless, despite how effectively victims carry out this strategy. They just won't stop. Regardless of responses, these bullies continue to taunt and torment.

No doubt, the predators are bully/victims. How angry they are or how much they want revenge will determine how long the bullying goes on. Unfortunately, the victim's reaction to this type of bully may have little or no effect. The bully/victim may get tired of not getting a reaction from the victim and stop—a good reason to always start with this approach. Alternatively, depending on the degree of anger of the bully, the bullying may continue indefinitely. A classic example is the James Brenton story told in chapter 9. Regardless of what James did, the group of bullies was determined to make him a social outcast and suffer because they were so angry. So what should the intended victim of this type of bully try next? The best strategy is to continue in the strategy already described. Tell the child not to react, not to give power to the bully. The child should avoid the bully as much as possible and hang out with friends in a group at school as much as possible. This is often a deterrent—bullies usually like to pick on kids who are alone. Suggest that children walk to school or sit on the bus with someone who can protect them. Lastly, they should seek out help from an adult they trust on the campus or at home. Reporting the bully to administration may be the only available solution to stop the behavior.

18

CLASSROOM-TESTED LESSONS

Work in the Home and in School

Think about a perfect world where everyone is polite and kind to each other. What a pleasant thought. No doubt, bullying couldn't and wouldn't exist in such a world. There would be no need to bully-proof children. They would be born into a world with perfect role-models as parents and would simply emulate them. There would be no need to even write this book. But, alas, our world is not perfect. Intolerance is a part of our real world. In fact, there are adults and children who can be mean, angry, and even hateful. So yes, we must bully-proof our children. We must prepare them to tolerate and cope effectively with all people and to strive to be the best they can be as people in order to make our world a better place (even if not perfect) for their generation and the next. Teaching our children tolerance is the foundation of any antibully program.

We will successfully bully-proof our children when we teach all children to be kind and tolerant of one another. Respect and acceptance of others is the cornerstone of tolerance. Accepting nothing less than respectful behavior from our children is the solution. The two units that follow are specifically designed to teach children early on how to get along and respect one another by promoting kindness, respect, and acceptance. Each unit consists of a series of lessons and activities that teachers can use in the classroom or parents can use in the home.

The first unit is entitled "Bee Kind: Buzzin' Together to Create a Nicer World." It consists of seven lessons for children in grades K–3. The unit's first lesson begins with reading the storybook *The Big Squeal*, to introduce the notion of teasing and its effect on children. In lesson 2, children agree to take a pledge to get along with each other. Lessons 3 through 7 encourage children to get along by using kind words, by not teasing or tattling, by being friendly and helpful, and lastly by solving conflicts with others. The unit ends with a poem that reinforces the concept that it is "your" responsibility to get along and be kind to others.

The next five lessons make up a unit entitled "Erase Bullying and Teasing," geared for children in grades 3–9. This unit also begins with a pledge—to erase bullying and teasing. Lesson 2 explains what bullying is all about, while lessons 3, 4, and 5 delve into empathy, coping strategies, and helping others who are teased. This unit also ends with a poem on kindness, as it brings home the message that it is your choice to be kind to others.

Each unit is designed to teach children life's important lessons that will help make the world a better place and at the same time send messages that will act to shield or bully-proof them:

Treat everyone with respect.
We get along when we are kind to each other.
It is up to us to choose to be kind.
Think about your words before you say them.
Kind words make us happy.
Mean words and acts hurt our feelings and bodies.
Treat others the way you want to be treated. That's called respect.
Think before you act.
You have a choice about how to act.
You are responsible for your actions.
We are all unique in our own way. It's okay to be different.
I can solve conflicts with words.
Hands are for helping not hurting others.
We need to help others who are not being treated nicely.
Bee cool if you are "picked on." Don't overreact to teasing/bullying.

BEE KIND: BUZZIN' TOGETHER
TO CREATE A NICER WORLD, AGES 4-8

Lesson #1: The Big Squeal

Background

The Big Squeal offers an opportunity for teachers, counselors, and parents to use literature not only to excite children about reading and teach important reading skills and character education, but also to help bully-proof children. It is the story of Nate, a little boy who is always "picked on" in school because he is different. He feels all alone and suffers in silence until everything changes one day when a special surprise visitor named Teddy comes to school. It is told in rhyme with lively illustrations, and children ages five to eight will chuckle with delight and surprise as Teddy's identity unfolds. Reading *The Big Squeal* with your child and class is a warm and delightful way to bully-proof children early on through teaching kindness and acceptance.

Expected Outcomes

Children will build empathy skills as they follow the plight of Nate at school. They will understand that it is everyone's responsibility to treat others with respect and to help others that are not being treated fairly.

Children Learn

It's okay to be different. We must not treat others unkindly just because they are different. We need to look for the good in others. There is a hero in all of us. It hurts feelings deeply when we tease others. We need to treat everyone with kindness.

Children learn about reacting to teasing. They should not overreact, because that can make it worse. Children will learn that they should help others who are being treated unfairly.

Introduction

Holding up the book cover, say: *Good morning boys and girls. I'd like you to meet Nate. The kids in his school loved to tease him. But when he was teased, he got so angry he almost flipped his top! How many of you have ever been teased? Did you ever feel like Nate? Let's see what happens one day when a surprise visitor comes to his school and changes everything.*
    Read the story.

Questions for Guided Discussion

1. Did Nate like going to school? Why?
2. Why did the kids tease him? Did he do anything to get himself teased?
3. Should someone be teased if they are different?
4. How did Nate feel about the teasing? How do you know?
5. Why did the kids finally stop teasing Nate?
6. Did Nate feel better when the teasing stopped? Why?
7. How did Teddy change things for Nate?
8. How did Nate become a hero?
9. When did you figure out that Nate was a pig? What clues in the story could have been hints?
10. Were the boys and girls in the school being kind to Nate? Do you think it was right for them to behave that way?
11. Did anyone help Nate? Why not? Is there anything that some of the students could have done to help Nate? Should they have helped?
12. What advice did Ms. Gail give Nate? Did it help?
13. How did Nate feel at the end of the story? How do you know?

Lesson

How many of you can think of a time when you were teased like this by other kids—called mean names or not been allowed to play with others? How did that make you feel? How many of you would like to put an end to all teasing here at _____ *school? Tomorrow we will talk about how to do that.*

Lesson #2: The Pledge: We Can Get Along

Background

We need to begin early on to teach children how to get along with others and treat others with respect by promoting kindness and acceptance in our young children.

Expected Outcomes

Children learn that there are things we can say and do to help us get along. Children will commit and pledge to get along with others.

Children Learn

Getting along means using kind words and acting friendly. It means helping others and solving problems with others. Tattling and teasing behaviors don't help us get along—they make us angry.

Introduction

Say: *How many of you have ever been teased? Called a name?*

Sometimes we get along and sometimes we don't. When we don't get along we fight, hit, kick, argue, yell, name call, or just say mean things by tattling or teasing or leaving others out. How does that make you feel?

But sometimes we use kind words and play and work together nicely—how do you feel then?

How many of you would like to feel happy all the time at school, with everyone getting along?

How many of you are willing to help make school a happy place by getting along with each other?

How many of you are willing to take a pledge (or make a promise) to get along here at _____ *(could be home or school)?*

When you take the pledge, you say it, you sign it, and then you do it. You promise to do what it says.

Are you ready to take the pledge and promise to get along with each other? Raise your right hand and repeat after me (one line at a time).

Bee Kind
We Can Get Along
Our Pledge

1. I use words to be kind to others.
2. I don't tattle on or tease others.
3. I am friendly and include others.
4. I use my hands for helping not hurting others.
5. I solve my problems with others.

Activities

1. Each student receives a picture of a bee outlined on a ditto.
2. Kids take the pledge, color their bee, and write (if they can) their names on it, to agree they will follow it. At the beginning of each lesson the kids say the pledge: repeating after the teacher or reading it if they can.
3. Create a class bulletin board titled "Bee Kind: Buzzin' Together to Create a Nicer World." Divide the bulletin board in half with two subtitles side-by-side: "We Can Get Along" and "It's All up to You." Put the pledge on one side (the children color the bees and write their names on them). Post the bees around the pledge. (The other side of the bulletin board will be completed at the end of the unit.)

Lesson #3: I Use Words to Be Kind to Others

Background

Children need to learn early on that their words affect others and if chosen carefully can help them get along with others. Teaching children to think about their words before they say them is important.

Expected Outcomes

Words have a strong impact on others. Children will learn that they are responsible for their words and they should select them carefully to be kind to others. Children will learn how to give compliments. In this way they are treating others with respect—the way they want to be treated.

Children Learn

Kind words make us feel happy. Using kind words helps us get along. Mean words make us feel angry and sad. Teasing words are mean words.

Introduction

Say: *Today we are going to talk about part 1 of our pledge. How can we use words to be kind to others? Remember that certain words, I call them kind words, can make us feel happy, while other words can hurt our feelings and make us feel sad and angry. We show respect for others when we use kind words because we are treating others the way we would like to be treated. If we can think about our words before we speak, we can choose only kind words that help us to get along with each other.*

Who controls the words that come out of your mouth? We need to stop and think before we speak—stop, think, and say. It's your choice of words that will help you get along with others. Now let's look at what the kind words are.

Part I: Kind and Mean Words

Say: *Let's make a list of kind words. What are the kind words we should use frequently?*

Prompt the kids with questions if necessary:

If someone does something to help us or says something nice to us, what do we say? [Thank you]

When someone says thank you, what do you say? [You're welcome]

If you'd like one of my cookies, do you say "gimme one"? What do you say? [Please]

If by accident I bump into you, what should I say? [Excuse me, or Sorry]

You want to get in front of someone on line—what do you say? [May I]

If someone is alone on the play yard, what could you say? [Come play with us]

Activities

1. Have the children practice using these words through role-play. Give two children a situation to act out and then reverse the roles. For example: Jessica and Tim are coloring. Jessica needs Tim's red crayon because hers is missing from her box. What should she say?

2. Discussion: Stop, think, and say your words. Review with children why we use kind words. Say: *Let's look at the difference between kind words and mean words. Kind words work like magic. Say them, and poof! They make us feel happy. They make people like us for being nice. They tell others we are caring and respectful. The teasing and tattling words—I call them the mean words—Make us angry and sad and tell others we are not very nice. They make others want to stay away from us. So why should we stop and think before we say anything?*

3. Game: Play "Thumbs Up" (for practice distinguishing kind and mean words). Directions: In response to statements, children put thumbs up if the words are kind words and thumbs down if the words are mean or teasing words. Discuss those phrases that may be less obvious to young children. Here is a sampling of phrases:

   You did a good job.
   You're a cry baby.
   May I help?
   That's mine!

Thank you for your help.
You can't do the trick.
Hurry up, slowpoke.
I can jump rope better than you.
Do it my way.
Would you like a cookie?
Your haircut is too short.
May I help?
I got a higher grade than you.
That's a weird hat.
You run slowly.
You look sad.
I bet you didn't win.
You play the piano well.
I'll share my candy with you.

Part II: Teaching Children How to Give Compliments

Model for children how to give compliments. Ask individual children to stand up and, as the adult, make eye contact, say their names, and pay them a compliment. Require that responses include "thank you" and "you're welcome."

Here are a few samples:
Tanner, you are a really good reader.
Bella, you did great on the math test. I'm proud of you.
Ashley, that is a beautiful blouse you have on.
Michael, I like the way you draw.
Bobby, you are so helpful to me when you put all the blocks away.

Discussion

Say:

What am I doing? [giving compliments]
What is a compliment? [when you say something nice about another person]

How does it make you feel when I give you a compliment? [happy, good]

Giving compliments is like giving presents—both the giver and receiver feel good!

Role-Play

Have the children practice giving each other compliments. Guide and evaluate students to make sure all steps are followed. (A child stands up and asks someone else to stand. Then the child makes eye contact, says the name of the child selected, and gives a compliment.) The children really enjoy doing this. Be sure to guide them to think about their words carefully and not just compliment on clothing or appearance (which of course is the easiest).

Activities

1. In a friendship circle practice giving compliments.
2. Compliment box: Let older children put written compliments in the box and then read them once a week.
3. Poster: Have kids make a poster listing the kind words. Title the poster "We Can Get Along If We Use Kind Words: Stop, Think, and Say 'It's Up to Me!'"
4. Distribute a ditto to younger children: "Kind Words Spread Happiness." Have the children creatively color happy faces and connect them to other happy faces.
5. Children look for opportunities to give each other compliments during the week. When they come back together, they discuss the compliments they received from others and how they made them feel.

Lesson #4: I Don't Tease Others

Background

Sometimes children say mean things to each other without even realizing how their words affect others. The "sticks and stones" slogan is difficult for young children to accept as the truth when someone calls them a name or makes fun of them. Children need to use words that are respectful to others.

Expected Outcomes

Children will learn that they are responsible for their words. They must think about them before they say them. They will learn the difference between kind and teasing words and their affect on others.

Children Learn

Kind words make us feel happy. Teasing words make us angry and sad. We make friends when we use kind words. Kind words help us to be liked by others. Kind words tell others we are caring, considerate, and respectful. Teasing words keep others away from us. Teasing words tell others that we are mean, selfish, and disrespectful.

Introduction

Say: *Today we're going to talk about part 2 of our pledge: I don't tease others.*

Lesson

Discuss with the children the effect of teasing words.

> How many of you have ever been teased? How does it feel?
> How would you describe kids who tease others?
> How would you describe kids who are complimenting you?
> Do you want to be friends with kids who use teasing words or kind words?
> Do we have a choice of which words to use?
> How can we make sure that we don't say something mean?

Activity

Play the game "Thumbs Up"

Directions

In response to statements, children put thumbs up if the words are kind words and thumbs down if the words are mean or teasing words. Discuss those phrases that may be less obvious to young children. Here is a sampling of phrases:

You did a good job.
You're a cry baby.
May I help?
That's mine!
Thank you for your help.
You can't do the trick.
Hurry up, slowpoke.
I can jump rope better than you.
Do it my way.
Would you like a cookie?
Your haircut is too short.
I got a higher grade than you.
That's a weird hat.
You run slowly.
You look sad.
I bet you didn't win.
You play the piano well.
I'll share my candy with you.

Lesson #5: I Don't Tattle on Others

Background

One of the biggest concerns of both parents and teachers alike is how to deal with tattling. "How do I get kids to stop tattling on each other?" "I am ready to tear my hair out." Tattling needs to be addressed because it is very divisive and is a way for kids to get others in trouble.

Children need to be rewarded and praised when they try to help a friend by telling and to be ignored when they tattle.

Expected Outcomes

Children will learn the difference between tattling and telling. They will understand that tattling does not help kids to get along with each other.

Children Learn

The intent of tattling is to get someone in trouble. Tattling makes us angry. Tattling is hurtful. The intent of telling is to help someone. Telling makes us happy. We are glad someone told. Telling is helpful.

Introduction

Say: *Today we're going to talk about part 2 of our pledge: "I don't tattle on or tease others." Teasing and tattling words don't help us get along.*

Begin with a brief discussion on tattling, since all children clearly have some sense about it.

Discussion Questions

What's a tattletale?
Has anyone ever tattled on you? (Allow a few students to tell their stories.)
Do you like tattletales?
How do you feel when someone tattles on you?

Lesson

Say: *I have a short story about a little boy, Tommy, who just couldn't stop tattling. Would you like to hear it?*
Read the story.

Tommy loved to tattle on the kids in the class. Every time someone did something he thought was wrong, Tommy would run up to Ms.

Tisch's desk and report it. "Miss Tisch, Jack is chewing gum. Ashley isn't doing her spelling words. Billy is out of his seat. James knocked over his blocks." Soon enough the kids in the class started calling him "Tommy Tattletale" and refused to play with him or have anything to do with him. Even Ms. Tisch would cringe when she saw Tommy coming. Tommy was very upset because of this and asked Ms. Tisch what to do because he didn't have any friends.

Stop and ask:
What do you think Ms. Tisch told him?
After a brief discussion, say: *Let's finish the story and find out.*

Ms. Tisch told Tommy that the reason he didn't have any friends anymore was because the kids were angry with him. "Kids don't like it when you tattle on them and get them in trouble, Tommy. Would you like it if the others did it to you?" answered Miss Tisch.

"No," said Tommy. So off went Tommy determined to not tattle anymore so the kids would like him again and play with him. He wanted his friends back. That day on the play yard Tommy came across Jessica near the slide. She was on the ground holding her knee and seemed upset. But Tommy didn't say anything because he was determined not to tattle anymore.

Stop and ask: *What's wrong here?*
Let the children conclude that Tommy should have reported it because this is not tattling. Ask why.

Explain the difference between telling and tattling. Say: *Telling is okay. We tell the teacher or parent or any adult when someone is hurt or there is a dangerous situation and someone could get hurt. Telling is helpful to another person and makes them happy you told. In this case, if Tommy told Ms. Tisch, it would help Jessica to get help with her hurting knee. Tattling is not helpful to the person. It only gets them in trouble and makes the person you tattled on angry.*

Activity

Play "Thumbs Up" to check for understanding and reinforce this lesson. Read a series of scenarios. After each scenario, have the children show thumbs up if it is telling and thumbs down if it is tattling.

Follow-Up

Reward and thereby encourage children to tell you things to help others. When children tattle, similarly ask them if they are telling or tattling and help them see it is tattling.

Lesson #6: I Use Hands for Helping Not Hurting Others

Background

Young children will often use their hands to express their feelings, protect their property, and get what they want. They may hit, push, or grab to this end. However, children need to learn early to use their hands and not their hands to express feelings.

Expected Outcomes

Children will learn that hitting or pushing is never acceptable behavior. They will understand that words are to be used to express them.

Children Learn

Hands are for helping not hurting. Hitting, pushing, or grabbing is never okay. We use our hands to help around home and in school.

Introduction

Say: *Today we are going to talk about part 4 of the pledge.*

Lesson

Guide the children in a discussion about how we use our hands appropriately.

How do you use your hands to help at home? At school?

How can you use your hands to get along with another?

How do you feel when someone hits or pushes you?

Have you ever felt like hitting someone? Did you?

Why shouldn't you hit someone when you get angry?

What should you do if someone gets you really angry?

What should you do if someone grabs a toy you are playing with?

Activity

Have the children draw an outline of their hands on a paper entitled "Helping Hands." On one hand, ask them to draw pictures or write things that they do at home to help. On the other hand, they should draw pictures or write things that they do in school to help. Post them on a bulletin board or refrigerator.

Lesson #7: I Can Solve Problems With Others

Background

Young children need to understand early on that conflicts are okay—they are a natural part of life. Life has its bumpy roads, and with the right tools they can smooth things out. Remember, for very young children, when conflict strikes their anger gets the best of them and too often they quickly resort to physical means to settle issues. Problem solving and conflict resolution are important skills to teach children early on so they are equipped with alternative means to settle conflict and get along with each other peacefully.

Expected Outcomes

Children will learn that they can use their words to resolve conflicts with each other. There is a myriad of things they can do. They do not have to push, hit, yell, or fight to settle a conflict.

Children Learn

How to identify and articulate the problem. How to resolve conflicts using a variety of strategies including talking it out, sharing, taking turns, using chance (rock, paper, scissors), compromising, walking away, and getting help. They will learn that problem solving requires calm and cool discussions and actions.

Introduction

Say: *How many of you have ever had an argument or fight with a friend? What happened? How did you settle it? What did you do? Did you yell at each other, walk away mad, or push or hit each other?*

How does it feel when you fight and argue with a friend, or with anyone, for that matter? Well, today we're going to talk about what to do when you have a problem or disagreement with a friend. Boys and girls, it's okay to disagree. It's okay to have a problem or conflict with others. That happens. What's important is that we learn to peacefully settle it and stay friends. Let's listen to a story of two close friends who got into a big argument and almost "blew" their friendship because they got so angry at each other.

Lesson

Read the story.

Cecil and Charlotte were friends forever and ever, or at least as far back as they could remember. Every morning Cecil would pick up Charlotte at her house and off they would go to Squeaky Elementary School. Oh, did I forget to tell you that Cecil and Charlotte were mice? This Friday morning as they were going past Farmer John's dairy farm on their way to school Charlotte noticed something on the ground. It was three one-dollar bills. They quickly picked them up and asked Farmer John if the money was his. He said no but that he would sell them three large chunks of cheese with the money. Excitedly they bought the cheese and ran as fast as they could to school.

Now, Cecil and Charlotte could barely contain themselves during second grade reading, thinking about lunch and the cheese. Finally, the lunch bell rang and Cecil and Charlotte went to their favorite hole outside Ms. Minnie's classroom. Each of them ate a large chunk of the cheese. But both were still hungry and there was only one chunk left. They started arguing over who would eat it and were yelling so loud that Ms. Minnie came out of her classroom to see what was wrong.

Stop reading. Start by guiding the children through the problem solving process. Ask children to define or state the problem: What is the problem that Cecil and Charlotte have to solve? [They only have one piece of cheese left and they both want it.]
Stop and discuss:

1. *What do you think Cecil and Charlotte should do?* Make a list of all the possible solutions. (You will be amazed at how many possible solutions they come up with and how creative the children will be. Accept all solutions.)
2. Ask them to evaluate each solution, giving the pros and cons of each.
3. Lastly, ask the class to vote on the best solution, then continue reading to find out what Cecil and Charlotte did.

Continue the story:

Ms. Minnie came out and told Cecil and Charlotte that they needed to stop fighting and solve their problem. Yelling was not the answer. They need to calmly and coolly talk it out. And that was exactly what they did. They both took a deep breath, counted to 10, and looked at all the possible ways to solve their problem and decided that the best one was to cut the chunk in half and to share the cheese. So off they squealed to the cafeteria, where Mr. Mickey cut the cheese into two even pieces. Ms. Minnie was very proud of her two little problem solvers. Cecil and Charlotte were also happy because they had settled their problem themselves without more arguing and both had full tummies now.

Role-Play

Children should be given practice solving problems. Invite children to role-play problematic situations by applying the problem-solving method. Guide the children by asking the three questions:

What is the problem?
What are possible solutions?
Which solution is the best?

Here are some "what if" scenarios to use:

1. Jessica and Abbey both want to take out the single copy of *The Big Squeal* from the library.
2. Ben tells his friend Tim, "You can't play with me."
3. On Valentine's Day the teacher handed out one box of crayons for every two students. The box that Tanner and Tobey got was missing a red crayon.
4. Only one seat is left at the lunch table. Marcus, Ashley, and Jack want to sit there.
5. James is using all the blocks in the block corner to build a huge castle. Jackson wants to play with them too.
6. Samantha borrows a pencil from Cecilia and breaks it.

Activities

1. Make a list of the solutions that are effective. Include sharing, taking turns, using chance (rock, paper, scissors), compromising, walking away, and getting help from an adult.
2. Model and have children give you examples of when they would use each solution. Let students practice these solutions in role-play.
3. Design a poster entitled "I Solved My Problem" and list all the strategies. Leave space in between the strategies so you can stick on happy faces (with children's initials on them). Once or twice a week have a reporting time (this could be your circle of friends time). Have children tell the class or family how they

solved a problem. They state the nature of the problem and what strategy they used. They then get to put a happy face with their initials on it on the poster next to the strategy they used. It's very important to reward and praise the children every time they solve a problem on their own to reinforce this behavior.

BEE KIND: BUZZIN' TOGETHER TO CREATE A NICER WORLD: SUMMARY LESSON

Use the poem for a summary lesson to review the concepts of the unit. Here, the students, where age-appropriate, can discuss its meaning, memorize it, or recite it.

Bee Kind
It's All Up to You

Beeing kind
Is all in your mind,
You can just choose to be nice
to all . . . even the mice.
It's not a matter of throwing the dice.
It's all up to you
To choose what you say,
And friendliness in the end will pay.
Just stand up tall as high as the sky,
Looking someone in the eye,
Smile and say hi.
Don't forget "Please," "Thank you," and "May I."
It's all up to you to choose what you do.
Try shaking hands, sharing, and giving too.
Beeing kind is all up to you.

Follow-Up Fun

Post this poem on the other half of the bulletin board begun in lesson 3. Have the children collect pictures from magazines, draw pictures, use clip art, or bring in photographs that show friendship and kindness toward others. Post the pictures around the poem.

ERASE BULLYING AND TEASING, AGES 8–12

Lesson #1: Take the Pledge

Background

At this age children have a great natural sense for justice. They don't like to see others mistreated but too often they get caught up in supporting this behavior because they want to be liked and accepted and are afraid if they don't support these inappropriate behaviors they might be ostracized. In order to bully-proof our children we must set a tone whereby respect and kindness is the only acceptable behavior, and teasing and bullying is shunned by all. When this is the goal that everyone works together toward, a peaceful, warm, and accepting environment results.

Expected Outcomes

Children will want harmony and kindness at their school. They will want to create an environment at school (or home) where everyone respects each other and treats each other in a respectful and helping manner. They will commit to working together to create this at their school (or home).

Children Learn

They are not alone, many of them are teased. The bullied or teased children really suffer and feel bad. They have a responsibility to help stop bullying. A school working together can put an end to bullying.

Introduction

Use a picture of someone overreacting or extremely angry, or show the picture of Nate on the cover of *The Big Squeal*. Say: *I'd like you to meet Nate. The kids in his school loved to tease him because when they did he would get soooooo angry. The way he reacted made it fun for the kids, so they kept doing it. Nate became a victim.*

Lesson

Here are some questions for discussions:

> Did you ever know someone like Nate? Tell us about him or her.
> How many of you have ever been teased? Or bullied?
> What is the difference?
> How did the teasing happen? (Have a few kids share their stories.)
> How did the teasing make you feel?
> How many would like to see teasing stop here at _____ school?

Say: *How many of you are willing to work together to stop bullying and teasing in our school? If we all pledge to stop teasing here at _____ school, what a pleasant and fun place it would be. How many of you are willing to take the pledge? I call it "The Erase Bullying and Teasing Pledge." Let's take a look at it.* (Have an overhead of it.)

Pledge to Erase Bullying and Teasing
> We won't tease or bully others.
> We will treat others with respect.
> We will include others who are being left out.
> We will help other students who are being teased or bullied.
> We will shield ourselves from teasing and bullying.

Have students recite the pledge together.

Activities

1. Go through magazines and find pictures that illustrate an aspect of the pledge. Cut them out, label which part of the pledge they demonstrate, and put them on the bulletin board.
2. Write an essay about a time when you were teased or bullied, how it felt, and what you did. Did it work?

3. Read a short story with two others in the class. Make a report on it. Summarize the story and message(s). Present it to the class. (See chapter 14 for a selection of stories.)
4. Put up a bulletin board with the pledge in the center. Have students sign their names around it.
5. Set up a box in the classroom and label it "Let's Erase Bullying and Teasing." Students place in the box slips of paper that start with the sentence, "I erased it by _____" (students describe an act or something they said to follow through on their pledge).

Lesson #2: Let's Learn About Bullying and Teasing

Background

In order to combat bullying, children must understand what this phenomenon is all about. There are many reasons why children tease and bully each other. It's important for children to explore the reasons for bullying so that, once they understand them, they can choose how to respond to it.

Expected Outcomes

Children will understand what bullying is all about. This knowledge will help them deal with this behavior and understand that it is unfair and has nothing to do with the victim.

Children Learn

Bullying covers a wide range of behaviors which can be physical, verbal, or emotional. It can include teasing, name-calling, hitting, pushing, or subtle behaviors like ignoring, spreading rumors, or excluding someone intentionally. What distinguishes teasing from bullying is that bullying is generally deliberate and hurtful behavior repeated over a period of time. Children learn that there are many reasons why people tease and bully others but behind them is often a control issue. The bully needs to feel powerful and know he can control others with his put-downs.

Introduction

Say: *Today we are going to learn about bullying and teasing. What is bullying? What is teasing? What is the difference? Why do people tease or bully others? This is important to understand so we know how to handle it.*

Solicit answers to these questions from the students and list them on the board (you will be surprised at all the answers).

Lesson

Through guided discussion list all the reasons why people bully or tease others:

1. Some students have been teased by others.
2. They don't feel good about themselves—they need to put others down. That makes them feel superior.
3. To get revenge—getting even with someone who has hurt or irritated them.
4. To belong—they think that they can become part of a group if they tease people the group dislikes.
5. To get attention.
6. Power—some students tease others in order to control others. They feel in control when their teasing causes others to react in certain ways.

Behind all these reasons seems to be the need on the part of the bully to feel powerful and in control. Whether it's because the bully doesn't feel good about himself, wants revenge or attention, or to just belong, his reward is the power he feels over someone when he can "push their buttons."

Activity

Interview a parent on the topic of bullying and teasing. Have they ever been bullied or teased? What happened?

Lesson #3: Building Empathy

Background

To most bullies their victims are faceless. They are unable to understand how others are feeling. They feel no guilt ridiculing or putting others down. Empathy is a trait they don't possess. For very young children meaness is often the road to get what they want. For the older child meaness is all about the affect it has on "me"—it empowers them. The victim in both cases is faceless.

Expected Outcomes

Children will learn to listen carefully and hear what is being said. They will be able to put themselves "in the shoes" of others. They will be able to empathize with others.

Children Learn

Children will understand how others feel as if they were their own feelings. They will learn how to be good listeners and to ask questions so they can understand others' feelings. They will learn how to support others.

Introduction

Start by showing children a variety of pictures of people feeling differently. Ask: *What are they feeling? What makes you feel that way?* Use a face chart with pictures of faces with different expressions and action pictures of people interacting. Have the children read their feelings by their expressions and actions.

Lesson

Explain to students what empathy is. Empathy is the ability to show that you know what it's like to "be in another person's shoes," that you truly understand how they feel. It isn't giving advice or sympathy, solving another's problem, or passing judgment. When we empathize, we listen, question, and show the other person with our words that we know how they are feeling. It is similar to "mirroring"—we are able to do this because we understand.

Demonstrate the technique for the group. Let the students come up with some scenarios:

Example:

JASON: I hate Jack!

TEACHER: What happened?

JASON: He always yells at me when I miss a basket! He calls me a wimp in front of the team! (angrily)

TEACHER: Boy, that must make you really angry!

JASON: Yeah! I want to kill him!

TEACHER: That's really embarrassing in front of the others.

JASON: Yeah, I want to crawl under a rock.

Discuss with the class what happened and its effect on Jason to ensure that the children understand. How did Jason feel?

Role-Play

After a few demonstrations by the teacher, have children role-play a variety of situations. Have one child act upset as the other empathizes. Evaluate.

Lesson #4: We Will Help Others Who Are Being Teased

Background

Bullying and teasing flourish on a campus that closes its eyes to it. Every person must have "zero tolerance" for this behavior. Everyone must make a contribution and commitment to creating a bully-proof environment. Students, staff, and parents must help those who are bullied. Bystanders who watch bullying going on and do nothing about it are as guilty as the bully.

Expected Outcomes

Children will understand that they have a responsibility to helping others who are being bullied if they want their school to be bully-free. Children will learn what to do to keep their campus safe from bullies. Children will believe that anyone who sits quietly and watches someone getting bullied is just as guilty as the bully himself.

Children Learn

They need to help others who are teased or bullied. They need to include others who are left out. Children will learn what to do, how to speak up or report bullying to adults.

Introduction

Take a survey of the class: If you saw someone being bullied:

1. How many of you would say something to the bully?
2. How many of you would walk away and ignore it?
3. How many of you would report it?

Write the results on the board.

Lesson

Begin a discussion on the topic of what to do when others are teased. Guided discussion questions:

How many of you have watched or seen others being teased?
How many of you know about someone who is teased by others?
How did you feel about it?
How many of you think you should do something?
What would happen if I as a teacher saw it or knew of it? Should I do anything? What? Why?
What would happen if no one on the campus did anything about it, and every child was allowed to pick on others?

Should everyone have an obligation or duty to do something about it when they know about it or see it? Why? Why not?

Activities

1. Make a list of things that can be done to help others being teased. Potential answers may include: tell the bully to stop, get the victim out of the situation, empathize with the victim, tell an adult, and so forth.
2. Role-play: Practice the different strategies in a variety of bully situations.

Lesson: #5: I Shield Myself (Coping Strategies)

Background

Children need to be educated as to how to respond to bully behavior. Giving children practice with these strategies will bully-proof children and prevent them from acting like victims. There are a number of strategies that a child may use to respond to bullies.

Expected Outcomes

Children will understand that bullies are looking for a reaction from their victims. This reaction is the reward for the bully. He or she feels powerful and in control of another when he or she can "push buttons." The key is to not give the bully a reaction. Children will learn that the best shield from a bully is acting cool.

Children Learn

Everyone has a choice of how to respond to a bully. There are ways to shield and protect themselves. They can ignore the bully, walk away, get help, or use humor. When children react with anger and tears (or any demonstration that the bully has gotten to them) the bully has won. He will be back. When they don't react or take the bait, the bully may look for someone who does—it's more enjoyable.

Introduction

Review that bullying is all about feeling powerful, about picking on someone the bullies feel they can control.

Lesson

Say: *Knowing that you have a choice on how to act, you can react the way the bully wants you to, with anger, tears, or sadness, or you can be cool.*

In a role-play, demonstrate the two worst reactions that children can have: acting hot and cold for the class. This translates into acting very angry by yelling at the bully to stop, then crying to show the cold response. Discuss what's wrong with each response. Why don't they work?

Tell the children that if the bully gets you angry, it's important to calm down before you react:

1. Take a breath.
2. Say to yourself (out loud for the class) "Calm down. Don't let him get to you. That's what he wants."
3. Stand tall and aloof and choose a strategy.

It's important to discuss body language and how that can make you look hot or cold.

Next, demonstrate a cool response. Discuss each strategy below and why it works. It is the child's choice to pick the strategy that works for them:

Ignore the teaser. Pretend he isn't there. Don't look at him, and keep walking. He'll probably try harder, but you keep ignoring the comments. This is especially good when strangers tease you.

Avoid the teaser: Just stay away from the teaser. Go to a different part of the playground.

Use humor: Laugh or make jokes about the teasing comments.

Agree with the teasing: Tell the teaser he's right . . . "My dress is ugly."

Just change the subject: Ignore the comment and start another
conversation or activity.

Assert yourself and calmly ask the person to stop: Tell the teaser
that you don't like being teased. Tell them how you feel. Tell
them to stop and what you plan to do if they don't stop. It's important to stress that these words be delivered calmly without
emotion in the voice. (This strategy should only be used with a
friend, not a stranger.)

Say: *The best shield or protection from a bully is yourself. You have
to believe in yourself, believe that you are a good person, a nice
and caring person who is special and unique. You have to be proud of
and comfortable with who you are. Carry this with you like a shield.
Then, only then, can you not worry about what some bully thinks.
Nasty, mean remarks bounce off your shield. Remember that the bully
will say anything that gets to you; it doesn't matter if it's true or not.*

Activities

1. Have all children role-play being a victim and being the bully.
   Try out the various strategies.
2. Children list their strengths, positive qualities, and talents, asking themselves, What am I good at?
3. Design a bulletin board entitled "Class 101 Is Special." Put a
   picture of all students and list various adjectives to describe
   their classmates.

Erase Bullying and Teasing: Summary Lesson

Use the poem for a summary lesson to review the concepts of the
unit where age-appropriate. Have the students study the words, interpret them, and memorize and recite them.

Bee Kind
It's All Up to You

Being kind

Is all in your mind,
You can just choose to be nice
to all . . . even the mice.
It's not a matter of throwing the dice.
It's all up to you
To choose what you say,
And friendliness in the end will pay.
Just stand up tall as high as the sky,
Looking someone in the eye,
Smile and say hi.
Don't forget "Please," "Thank you," and "May I."
It's all up to you to choose what you do.
Try shaking hands, sharing, and giving too.
Being kind is all up to you.
So take the pledge now,
Later it will be a bow
To get along and bee kind
And no doubt you will find,
When you start
To act and speak with your heart,
How happy all of us will bee,
Including you and me!
Tall, short, skinny, or fat
In a dress, pants, or hat,
Men, women, and children too
Being kind is all up to you.

PART 5

A PROACTIVE APPROACH
FOR PREVENTION

There is no doubt that an ounce of prevention is worth a pound of cure in the problem of bullying. The best thing that both parents and schools can do is to be proactive from the moment of birth and the moment children enter school in addressing the issue. Parents and teachers must have as part of their child-rearing practices and curriculum the teaching of basic life skills (including problem solving, being assertive, handling anger, and resolving conflict) to raise citizens that can and want to live in a peaceful and respectful world. They must create learning environments for children to thrive in and grow up to be caring, loving, and resilient individuals. Although we may not be able to create a "perfect" world where *all* children treat each other with respect, we certainly can attempt to teach all children to be kind and strong enough so they don't become bullies or victims.

19

CREATE A BULLY-PROOF ENVIRONMENT

What does a bully-proof environment for children look like? Imagine a place, a very peaceful place, where children are kind to each other and adults respect each other. No bullies or victims are allowed to be part of this landscape. And of course without them, the environment is a healthy, supportive one for all children. Is it possible to create such a utopia? Probably not. But if we advise children to shoot for the moon, they may just get the stars.

IN THE HOME

Parents play the most significant role in creating a bully-proof environment. The home shapes children in those early crucial years for the later years. What happens during those preschool years is a major determinant of whether bullies or victims will be sent to school later on. Parents are children's primary teachers in those first four to five years. As role models, they will be copied and imitated by the children. Investing a lot of love and involvement with the child will serve as the foundation of a bully-proof house. The successful by-products will be children who are self-confident, nonaggressive, and compassionate. They are unlikely to grow up to be bullies or victims.

What should the home environment look like so that such children may emerge? What parenting practices should be part of it? What can parents do to create it? The bully-proof home environment:

Is Warm and Accepting

A warm and accepting environment promotes feelings of security and self-confidence. In this environment children are taken seriously; they are listened to and treated respectfully. As a result they feel important. Clearly defined limits are set and communicated so that children feel secure. They know what is expected of them and what is not allowed. Permissiveness is not the same as warmth.

Parents need to gradually introduce children to anxiety-provoking situations and experiences. Forcing children to do things that are frightening gives rise to mistrust and insecurity. They play games like peek-a-boo with infants so they learn to enjoy the disappearance and reappearance of the parent. They leave the toddler for short periods of time to start with and gradually lengthen the period of time. They do not sneak out.

Spontaneous hugs and warm feelings are frequently and openly expressed. There need not be a reason other than to send a message "I love you for you." This is especially important when children misbehave. Parents must be careful not to withdraw their love. Their love must not be based on what children do but on who they are. It must be unconditional. When children are disciplined, parents must be calm and firm to let children know that their behavior is unacceptable. Rejecting a child by angrily saying, "You are a brat" when they crayon on a wall sends the wrong message. Instead, in a firm and calm manner, parents address the behavior. "You need to use the crayons on the paper not the wall. Please clean the wall."

A bully-proof environment is optimistic. Everyone is encouraged to focus on strengths rather than weaknesses and to speak positively about others. The glass is always half full rather than half empty.

Sets Limits for Behavior

Effective parenting practices positively shape children's behavior. Parents need to take control and set limits for behavior. When they don't, children keep testing to find those limits and we see out-of-control kids who very well may exhibit bully behaviors. Children want to know where their limits are: what is allowed and what is not. When they understand where the limits are, they feel more comfortable; there is no need to constantly test to find out. They know what to expect. Their world is not as stressful as it is when faced with the unknown. They feel more secure and confident.

Promotes High Self-Esteem

Self-esteem refers to how one feels about himself or herself. Self-esteem increases when children feel "accepted." When they are taken seriously and respected in the family, they feel good about who they are. Approval and attention should be given at every opportunity. Encouragement and kind words motivate children to cooperate and meet challenges head on. When children hear their parents talking about their positive feelings they know they are special. Self-esteem is fostered when parents use praise. Any strengths and accomplishments of children should be recognized. Put-downs, sarcasm, and ridicule have no place in the home for raising healthy children. Rather, they lower feelings of self-worth and make children feel badly about themselves and their capabilities.

When children feel that they know how to successfully cope with and master their environment, their self-esteem is further enhanced. Their self-confidence increases with each and every successful experience. Parents should give children tasks and chores that are a bit challenging but designed so they can be successful— whether it's just putting toys away or cleaning their room. It takes a lot of patience sometimes to sit back, watch your child fumble over a task, and not do it for them. But in the end, children learn to say, "Gee, I did good work. I did it all by myself!"

Similarly, when children are confronted with conflicts and problems, support them as they seek solutions independently. Frequently doing things and making decisions for children undermines their self-confidence. It tells children that they can't do it themselves. The more situations they can handle independently and successfully, the more competent and happy they will be. Similarly, giving children choices is empowering, bestowing on them a sense of independence and control. Even simple decisions such as, "Do you want beans or squash for dinner?" or "Do you want to wear this dress or these slacks?" are great for young children. Complimenting them on their choices reinforces their decision-making skills.

Enroll children in activities where they can develop skills, have fun, and interact with peers. Athletics, music, and dance are just a few examples. Focus on what they are interested in and help them set goals. Focusing on the importance of trying regardless of the outcome develops in children an "I can" feeling. Always encourage children to do their best and tolerate frustration. Our acceptance and love in the face of nonmastery promotes this.

Encourages Open Communication and the Expression of Feelings

Children learn from watching Mom and Dad that all feelings are okay. They learn that feelings are expressed with words and not meant to be acted on. Anger, sadness, joy, and jealousy are all accepted and discussed openly. Everyone is an active and interested listener. When we inquire about children's feelings and listen carefully, we send a message that they are special to us. Young children are often scared by ideas of monsters, death, and so forth. Parents need to let them know that these fantasies and feelings are normal. When accepted, children are more likely to talk to parents about their fears and thoughts and not be so worried. Even as teens, children need to know that their awkward thoughts and feelings are normal and okay. Reassurance by parents when children get anxious or are upset sends a message that they will get through it and these feelings will pass. Staying calm when children scream, cry, or panic makes children feel safe and optimistic that these feelings will go away. Criticizing, denying, or blaming children for feeling anxious or upset will close down communication channels. Statements like: "I love you. Most people your age get upset by it and get through it. Sometimes it feels like nothing will help, but the feeling will pass and things will be fine again," will keep communication gates open.

Models and Teaches Social Skills

A home that explains and shows children how to stand up for themselves, get along with others, and deal with problems and conflicts bestows valuable gifts that will benefit children their entire life. Parents, as their children's primary teacher in those preschool years, should strive to explain the real world and how they fit in, in language that children comprehend. Parents need to look at themselves and ask if their words mirror their behavior. Explaining to young children the importance of treating others the way we want to be treated is great as long as parents act kind and compassionate in their own interactions with the children and with others. As parents we need to model by our behavior those social skills we want our children to learn.

Assertiveness

Children need to learn to ask for what they want, say no, and stand up for themselves. Parents must teach them early on that they can use their words to get what they want. They don't have to act aggressively and attack another verbally or physically. When they start with the word: "I" and *not* "you," the end result is often an assertive and not an aggressive response. The three-step rule is practiced, and everyone uses it in the house. Children are taught to:

Describe what they don't like,
Tell how they feel about it, and then
Tell what they want to see happen.

When children grab toys from others, rather then yell or grab it back, the other children are encouraged to use their words. "I don't like it when you take my toy without asking. I was playing with it and I want it back." Of course, like any of the other social skills, the best learning experience is watching parents model this behavior. Moreover, it is so important that children be allowed to interact with parents in an assertive way. A dictatorial parenting style stifles assertiveness in children. Instead, they learn early on to be controlled by others.

Problem Solving

To raise problem solvers, parents need to give children problems to solve. They need to communicate that problems are just challenges life presents to all of us. They are meant to be faced and not avoided. It's how we deal with them that is important. Parents should routinely demonstrate an effective problem solving method. Teach children to follow a model:

State the issue (what is the problem?).
Think about all the possible solutions.
Evaluate the solutions.
Choose the best solution and act.

Use daily events as opportunities. Problem solve out loud in front of five-year-old Connor:

What should we have for dinner tonight? Let's see. I have hamburgers in the freezer. We could send out for Chinese food; we could just go out for dinner; or I could go to the store and do some grocery shopping. Dad will probably be too tired to go out when he comes home. I'm too tired to go shopping now—it's already 5:30. The hamburgers will never defrost in time. I think we'll just send out for Chinese food.

Depending on the age of the child, enlisting the help of children early to share the problem solving is great practice for them. Children love to play "what if" games, which is a great way to foster problem solving skills.

Conflict Resolution

Again, parents need to develop in children an understanding that conflict is a natural part of life. There are times when we just don't agree with family members or friends. Disagreements, arguments, and fights are settled with words and not hands. Children learn to share, take turns, and use other techniques for settling conflicts. Chapter 20 explains in detail how to teach children this skill.

Friendship Skills

In the bully-proof home, children are exposed to other children their own age quite young and on a frequent basis. Parents can join mommy-and-me classes with their toddlers even though there is probably more parallel play then anything else. But that is okay. The children still get used to being around others. As they get older, they learn to get along when offered interactive experiences. Parents should monitor children's play and reward positive interaction. Being friendly is something that is encouraged and taught. Parents model these important skills for the child. Children with a strong network of friends are much less likely to be targeted as victims than children who are "loners." Chapter 21 discusses friendship: the making and keeping of friends.

Encourages Siblings to Cooperate—A Learning Opportunity

Sibling rivalry. Just mention the words and watch the grimace come across the face of most parents with two or more children in the household. I can't tell you as a counselor how many times I have had the words uttered, "All I want is peace in the house. They (children) are driving me crazy with all the fighting. I've tried everything, nothing I do seems to be working."

Sibling rivalry can be downright annoying. On top of that, often parents feel disappointment in themselves in being unable to create happy and harmonious relationships in the home all the time. They feel inadequate when they are at a loss as to what to do so their children will stop fighting. But this is probably their biggest mistake, since parents' best strategy is *not* to do anything. Most of the hostility and jealousy that brothers and sisters develop toward one another is normal, as long as the arguing, fighting, and teasing is interspersed with getting along and interacting peacefully. It's when it becomes excessive, and all they do is fight and argue that some plan needs to be put into action.

Since in most instances, sibling rivalry is a competition for parents' love, attention, and approval, the key is not to give it to either child during a conflict. Do nothing? Yes. The best way to handle it is to stay out of it. You would be amazed at what kids can resolve if parents don't intervene. However, be sure the kids are evenly matched first. If not, we will talk about some other strategies. Assuming that the kids are both evenly matched in their ability to stand up for themselves, ignore their minor fights. Above all, never make a judgment about who is right and wrong. Remember parental approval, love, or attention given to one and taken from the other only leads to more sibling rivalry. Not to mention tattling behaviors you might be inadvertently encouraging when you decide to be judge and jury. When you judge and take a side, you have a winner and a loser. The loser will inevitably be angry with the winner. Basically, you are setting the kids up for rounds two, three, and so on.

Instead this is a wonderful opportunity to teach children conflict resolution and problem solving skills. The following script can be used with most arguments:

- Ask the questions: *What's the problem? How can you guys fix it?* Make it their problem.
- After the problem is stated, tell them, *It takes two to fight and I know you can both work the problem out. Let me know how you solve it.*

- Reward them with approval or a treat when they tell you how they solved the problem. *Thank you both for solving your problem on your own.* Any creative and safe solution that works for both of them should be praised. The key here is recognizing cooperation and reinforcing successful problem solving. We have a win-win situation because the children resolved it between them. There is no loser to get angry.
- Continue watching for those moments when they are playing nicely and praise them: *You guys are really cooperating and getting along without fighting. Good for you.*
- What if the children continue arguing and fighting and are unable to solve their problem or they are not evenly matched? Allow the children time to calm down and then mediate to demonstrate to the children how to problem solve. Say: *It seems that the two of you are unable to solve the problem by yourselves. Would you like some help? First of all, the two of you seem very angry at each other. You can't solve problems when you're angry, so let's take a time-out.* When you feel they have sufficiently calmed down (after about 10–30 minutes), have them come together. Then, follow the mediation script outlined in chapter 20. This may be necessary to do a few times until the children get the hang of it. In the beginning, there is an investment of time needed. Although, it's easier to take the short cut by acting like the judge and issuing a verdict, in the long run you are teaching children valuable skills.

IN THE SCHOOL

Since schools are a primary place where bullying and aggressive behaviors occur (because children spend approximately six hours daily interacting with other kids) it is crucial that all schools have an effective program to prevent and reduce bullying on the campus. Research indicates that where schools have a complacent attitude toward bullying, burying their heads and looking the other way and not enforcing rules against it, bullying does become a part of the landscape. Where there is a schoolwide commitment against bullying, bullying not only can be prevented, but also can be significantly reduced where a pattern has already developed.

There are several things that a school can do to create an environment that is free of bullies and victims. The focus in the school must be on raising awareness about bullying, developing strong social norms against bullying, and supporting all students in their quest to stop bullying. Everyone, including the students, parents, teachers, principal, office staff, cafeteria workers, and campus supervisors, should be involved and committed to an antibully policy.

As in the home, a bully-proof environment requires a warm and accepting tone in the classroom and throughout the school. Open and honest communication is encouraged, and social skills continue to be taught and reinforced. Clear expectations are set, and rules are enforced. The staff incorporates ongoing education on getting along and bullying as part of the curriculum. The staff and students make a commitment to fight bullying and aggressive behaviors. How do we do this? What does this school look like? The bully-proof school environment:

Is Warm and Accepting

This is a school where the feeling of community becomes obvious no matter what part of the campus a person visits. There is a lot of involvement among staff, pupils, and parents. Adults lead by example in and out of the classroom. They model behavior that is respectful to all. They are kind, empathetic, and encouraging individuals. Teachers look for the strengths and talents in their pupils and are quick to give positive praise. They are supportive and helpful and expect students to act similarly toward their classmates. Character education is part of the daily curriculum as children learn what it means to be respectful, honest, kind, and caring toward others. Long lists of behaviors are made that demonstrate each of the character traits. Art projects and role-playing activities are built around them.

The teachers are continually looking for model student behaviors that they can recognize and praise out loud so that others repeat them. When Ms. Brooks sees Jason helping Jenna clean up, she points this out (with praise for Jason) to the class. A star goes up on a chart to record good behavior. When there is a clear-cut bully situation the teacher is quick to give empathy to the victim. Student-of-the-week and student-of-the-month programs are incorporated in the classroom and at assembly programs to spotlight students' kindness toward others. Schoolwide contests and posters spotlight positive and responsible behaviors. All adults on campus watch for behavior that they can reward with "caught-in-the-act" coupons. Spirit and schoolwide activity days promote the feeling of community and pride in the school. Children learn that we are alike in that we are all human and have feelings but are also very different from one another. This is what makes each one of them special. Their individuality is respected; it's nice to be their own person and be different from the crowd. They accept and tolerate differences in each other. Others aren't excluded because they are different.

Has Clear Expectations and Enforces Rules Consistently

The teacher sets clear expectations for behavior. Kindness and respect is everyone's responsibility. No teasing or mean words or acts are allowed. Children are expected to help others who are picked on and to include students if they are left out. In fact in many classrooms teachers take input from the class as to what the five important rules should be. The rules are posted, discussed, and consistently enforced. Consequences for breaking the rules are explained to the students. These may include no recess, a detention after school, writing a "sorry" note, and so forth. While the focus here is on positive behavior, children are held accountable as consequences are quietly doled out. If children push each other, the teachers call them to their desk and give them a detention slip as they quietly say, "Your hands are for helping not pushing." Teachers use coupons to monitor student behaviors. When they are given out for a kind act, they make an announcement and explain why to the class.

The principal visits each classroom and reviews school rules on the playgrounds and in the hallways and cafeteria and what the consequences are for breaking them. Supervision by teachers and parents is plentiful. They are trained in what to look for and how to respond when they see teasing or bullying behaviors. When a bully situation does come up, the principal is quick to confront the bully and invite the parent in for a conference. The victim is totally supported and trained to defeat the bully. Other students are encouraged to help victims with an anonymous tip (by placing a note in the office tip box) or simply by confidentially reporting it to a teacher.

Educates Everyone on How to Get Along and How to Stop Bullies

Beginning in kindergarten, all children are taught a curriculum rich in social skills. They are taught to be kind to each other. Lessons on conflict resolution and problem solving are given in every classroom. An emphasis is placed on replacing aggressive behaviors with assertiveness. Activities such as the friendship circle, cooperative learning projects, and role-playing are fun ways for children to learn to get along. Age-appropriate literature is selected that teaches and delivers important messages on acceptance and kindness.

This continues up into the third grade, when more complex information is delivered. Children develop an understanding of the whole phenomenon of bullying and teasing. From third grade through junior high school, children learn the what, how, and whys about bullying and how to cope with bullies. Stories are read that shed light on this topic so children know how to handle it and step forward to help others.

Building empathy skills remains a strong focus of the curriculum for all grade levels. Teachers of younger children hold up pictures of children's faces asking the class how they feel so that children learn to identify and describe emotions. With the older children, pictures of conflicts or stressful situations are shown, to promote discussions on resolution. Role-playing is fun and good practice for handling these situations. The classroom-tested lessons described in chapter

18 are used. The whole school participates in a character education program as children learn about respect, kindness, integrity, and honesty. Fun projects, contests, and activities are created to foster these qualities.

Children take a pledge and make a commitment to stop mean and aggressive behaviors. At all grade levels the focus is on acceptance, respect, and getting along. In the early grades, getting along is a major theme. Children promise to use kind words; not to be mean, tattle, or ridicule others; not to hit or kick; to resolve conflicts with words; and to help others who are being mistreated. In the upper grades, the commitment shifts to promises to help erase bullying. Children pledge not to bully, to help others who are being bullied, and to include those who are being left out.

20

TEACHING CONFLICT RESOLUTION

A Valuable Tool

Conflict resolution is the essence or heart of the bullying issue. Bully-proofing children successfully demands that they learn these skills. Teaching these skills to children at home and in school is the best proactive approach to the prevention of bullying. Moreover, it is also a powerful intervention. When children learn how to effectively deal with conflict, it eradicates the need for them to employ bully and victim behaviors.

Children need to understand early on that conflicts are okay. They are a natural part of life. We all have our different wants and needs. We all see the world through different eyes. And it is because of this that we will and do challenge each other. But the "bumps" in the road of life can be smoothed out with the right tools. It is the job of the important adults in their lives to give children the tools that will successfully take them through the bumpy times with others.

For very young children, when conflict strikes, their anger gets the best of them and too often they quickly resort to physical means to settle issues. Problem solving and conflict resolution are important skills to model and teach children early on so they are equipped with alternative means to settle conflicts and get along with each other peacefully. All children need to be shown how to 1) deal with angry feelings, 2) problem solve, and 3) assert themselves. Both parents and teachers play significant roles in guiding children to attain these skills.

FIRST: SOME CHILD DEVELOPMENT

Understanding where children are in terms of developmental stages helps us maintain realistic expectations for children's behaviors and set realistic schedules for teaching them how to deal with conflict. While arguing and teasing may represent a normal developmental stage at one age, it may not at another. Two-year-olds hit, push, and grab, while older children tease or are verbally abusive to each other at times. Concern regarding this behavior should rise when the degree to which it occurs becomes excessive in the older child. Intervention strategies are needed before it becomes a pattern.

Aggression and fighting are normal responses in very young children when they feel their space invaded or safety or property threatened. Very close to the surface, aggressive and hostile behaviors emerge quickly when they feel a need to protect themselves. In their mind's eye they are reacting in a self-defense mode. Children up to the age of three tend to be impulsive, easily irritated, and action-oriented because their control systems are still immature, and they are inarticulate when it comes to their feelings. Unable to express their feelings with words, they will act out how they feel. While the first reaction of a two-year-old in response to settling a conflict over a toy is to strike the other child and grab the toy, a four-year-old is at least some of the time likely to argue about it first.

Between the ages of three and seven, children mature significantly in their ability to control their aggressive behaviors. With more words and vocabulary available to them, they don't have to resort to violent behaviors to express their anger. By the time children reach the ages of eight or nine, they should be able to control their aggressive behaviors although some brief, intense arguments may still occur.

THE PARENT'S JOB: ROLE MODEL

> *"Modeling is not the best way to teach. It is the only way to teach."*
>
> —Albert Schweitzer

Remember, as parents, that children are watching and imitating all your behaviors. No matter what you tell them they should do, it's what you do that will have the strongest impact. Therefore, when it comes to handling conflict, children will learn a great deal by observing and following the lead of their parents. Parents who are on overload and lose it when conflict strikes, will teach children to respond in a similar manner. Therefore, it's up to parents to ensure children are raised in a peaceful, nonviolent, and nonaggressive environment. Children should not be exposed to a high level of arguing, conflict, and aggressiveness between parents. When they are, the two most common outcomes are raising overly aggressive children who are at great risk for becoming bullies or children who are withdrawn and unable to deal with conflict and go to extremes to avoid it at all costs. Unable to assert themselves, they are at a greater risk to become victims of others. Parents who discuss and talk out problems in a mature and healthy manner are modeling exactly those problem-solving skills they want their children to learn.

ANGER MANAGEMENT:
DEALING WITH ANGRY FEELINGS

Anger management is a prerequisite to learning how to resolve conflicts. Until a person is able to control their anger, they are not ready to problem solve. So too with children. A very angry child must calm down first so good judgment is not clouded. Teaching children how to express all feelings constructively begins with sending them a clear message that all feelings are okay. Children need to understand that that they are responsible for their own feelings and actions. They can control their reactions to others. No one can make them angry. Only they can allow themselves to get angry. They can choose to ignore another's words and not to do anything at all. It is their choice not to feel angry or hurt (and not let their buttons get pushed). If they are going to automatically get upset when someone insults them, they are giving the other person power over them—

power to hurt them! If someone does make them angry, they can control their reaction to it. They win the game when they don't react like a victim. Play the "Sticks and Stones Challenge" game so children get used to being insulted.

Children should be encouraged to express all feelings with words. Very young children without the vocabulary should have their feelings translated from their actions or reflected back to them by parents so they begin to make the connection between words and feelings. When a child is crying in a store because Mom will not buy him or her a toy, Mom can say, "I'm sorry, but Momma isn't buying toys today. I know you are feeling angry and sad about that."

Later on, when children have the words, they should be taught to express their anger with their words in a calm fashion. Role-playing different scenarios (see a list at the end of this chapter) helps children to practice using words to express feelings and to assert themselves. Parents and teachers should always demonstrate and model the appropriate behaviors first in a role-play before having the children do it. Praise children when they successfully respond.

Lastly, remember parents must be the strong role models demonstrating on a daily basis for children the appropriate way to handle these feelings. When parents can express their own anger in a calm and controlled manner, so too will their children. Saying firmly and calmly to children, "I am very angry that you have used crayon on the wall. That is not okay. I need you to clean it immediately," sends a clear message to them on how to act when they get angry. We know that parents are neither perfect nor super robots, and certainly their anger can get intense enough to the point that they feel like they are going to "blow their top." That's okay to feel that way. But what parents do at this point is all-important. If you start screaming and yelling, getting nasty, or throwing things at others in response to the intense anger you feel, you as a parent are modeling for children how to be out of control when you get angry enough. Not a good thing unless you want your child to act this way.

ANGER MANAGEMENT STRATEGIES

Teaching children to control their feelings is next. You can show children how to cool down when they're angry, but if you cannot follow them teaching these strategies is fruitless. Modeling is, as usual, the most effective tool. A variety of ways to manage angry feelings and cool down are out there to choose from. Sometimes time is enough to allow the intensity of the anger to pass. Time-outs for young children often provide a way to help them cool down when they are out of control. Whichever strategy or combination of strategies works for you and your child is fine as long as it is a nonviolent means.

It is important to identify, model, and practice these strategies with children when they are not angry. Once they learn and practice them, hopefully they will use them well when they do get angry. Identify and practice a variety of strategies to deal with angry feelings—things that they can do and say to themselves to remain "cool." It is ideal if children are able to choose the technique that they are most comfortable with. Here are some examples:

1. Walk away and take time away from whatever or whoever is bothering you.
2. Do something that you enjoy to get your mind off it . . . maybe reading a book or favorite magazine.
3. Use positive self-talk. When tempted to get violent: Take a deep breath, tell yourself to count to 99. Tell yourself things like: "Stay calm and cool." "Talk, don't hit." "Stop and think before you act."
4. Think about or focus on other things.
5. Provide the child with an alternative way to ease anger like hitting a punching bag or pounding clay.
6. Express how you feel assertively (see pages 179–181) if it is a safe situation to do so (you are angry with a friend or parent not a stranger).

Model for children each of these strategies in a role-play first. With another adult, or a student volunteer, demonstrate hot, cold, and cool responses to nasty attacks. Acting hot (or really angry) usually makes the children laugh. When you act cold (or fearful, intimidated, or sad) the children usually also laugh. When you act cool, students can clearly see the benefits. This is also a chance to demonstrate how to calm yourself down with the strategies above before you decide how you want to react. Children learn that being cool is the only behavior that will get them respect. They can see how silly they can be viewed by others when they act hot or cold. Students should follow this up with role-play and practice.

TEACH CHILDREN PROBLEM SOLVING

Once children are calmly able to accept conflicts and face them as a challenge, they are ready to effectively learn problem solving. It's only when conflict is viewed as something "bad" that children have difficulty getting to this stage. Instead their anger gets the best of them; they "blow up" and deny or refuse to deal with the conflict rather than face it head-on to resolve it.

When we teach our children the tools for problem solving or resolving conflicts (because they are basically the same) we bestow on children some very precious gifts: positive self-esteem, an attitude of respect for all people, and the life skills needed to get along with others. These children become confident, assertive, responsible, and caring individuals capable of rising to any challenge later in life. We can use daily life events as opportunities to teach children the problem solving steps. Let's look at a common example and how to apply the problem-solving steps:

Example

A child is upset, as Mom declares it's time to go to bed.

Problem-Solving Steps

1. Define the problem objectively without placing blame. When we place blame, we teach children to look outside themselves

for a solution. Blame only puts the responsibility for the problem on someone else. The problem here is: It is 8 P.M. on a school night and the child doesn't want to go to sleep.

2. Listen, accept, and mirror back children's feelings. This encourages children to talk openly about their feelings. This also demonstrates for children how to actively listen to others. So when you say, "It sounds like you are angry at me because it is time to go to bed and you don't want to," you are acknowledging and accepting their feelings. Children know you care about their feelings and you think their feelings are important.

3. Brainstorm solutions for the problem with child. If this is a problem two children share or that you and your child share, it's important to put your heads together to work it out. If the child is having difficulty coming up with solutions, suggest a variety of solutions. The solutions can be very creative. Both parties contribute to the possibilities. Make a list of possible solutions: the child can stay up; the child can go to bed; the child can stay up later and go to school late the next morning; the child can stay up later past eight o'clock on another night when school isn't the next day, and so on. All solutions offered should be accepted.

4. Encourage the children or parties to the conflict to evaluate each solution and pick the one that both parties "can live with." They should examine the pros and cons of each solution and agree to pick one. It should be a win-win situation for both.

A Peace Table

A peace table is a great opportunity for children to come together to practice and master these skills. Set up a table or space in the home or classroom where kids can go to resolve conflicts. The peace table should have a clear set of rules posted that all parties agree to follow when they come to the table.

The Rules:

Listen politely.
Do not interrupt.
No put-downs, name-calling, or blaming.
Tell the truth.
Follow five steps to solve the problem:

1. Define the problem: What is the problem?
2. Brainstorm solutions: What are possible solutions?
3. Evaluate the solutions: What are the pros and cons of each?
4. Choose the solution: Which is the best solution for both of you?
5. Take whatever actions are agreed to.

MODEL PROBLEM SOLVING WITH MEDIATION

An effective starting point is to model problem-solving skills by mediation:

Step 1: Identify the Problem

Please start by each of you telling what happened, one person at a time. Please listen without interrupting or blaming anyone. Summarize their words: *John, you were playing with the racecar, and Tanner came and took it from you. Then, Tanner, you hit John when he took it back. The problem is you both want to play with it.*

Express "I" feelings: *How do you feel about this problem? Please begin with "I feel _____ because _____."*

Summarize their words: *John, you feel angry because Tanner took the red fire engine from you and hit you. Tanner, you are angry because John took it back and you want to play with it.*

Step 2: Brainstorm Solutions

What can we do to solve the problem? You both want to play with the car?

List all the possible solutions on paper, or blackboard. Suggest any that you can think of too and add to the list (i.e., we can take turns, play together with it, etc.).

Step 3: Evaluate Solutions

Which solutions are fair to both of you? Which is your choice? Remember, you both must agree on the same choice.

Step 4: Pick a Solution and Take Action

Have each child in his own words tell what they are agreeing to and will do.

Summarize their words: *You have both agreed to take turns playing with it. John will play with it for the first 10 minutes of recess. When the timer goes off, Tanner will play with it for the last 10 minutes.* Then say: *Thank you for working together to solve this problem. I know you will both follow the plan. If you have any further problems, you can talk them out together or come to me for help.*

Make a game of it. It's important to practice these skills. In the home or in the classroom, set up hypothetical situations that involve common conflicts between children and role-play the steps to resolve the conflict. Here are a few examples: 1) you both want to play with the same toy; 2) you both want to watch different television shows; 3) you bump into someone by accident. Make a list of general solution strategies that everyone can use and keep adding to them. Children must constantly be reminded of alternative and peaceful ways to resolve conflicts:

1. Taking turns (two children fighting over something)
2. Sharing
3. Apologizing (one child hurt another's feelings)
4. Postponing (talk about the problem at a later time)
5. Avoiding (one person could decide that it's not worth it to continue the conflict and give in to the other person's position)
6. Compromise (both parties may give something up to resolve the problem)

7. Humor (joking with the person in a friendly way)
8. Abandoning (if it looks like you and your partner are not getting anywhere—just walk away)
9. Using chance (rock, paper, scissors)
10. Seeking help (Encourage this, mediation, especially when children are younger)

However, as soon as workable and safe, step back and let the children work out problems.

In the beginning, have the kids take their time and make sure they go through each problem-solving step. Once they have internalized the steps, they can skip to offering solutions if it is clear they understand the problem.

TEACHING CHILDREN ASSERTIVENESS

Children will often react to conflict aggressively because they do not know how to "talk it out." Instead, they "fight it out" because they lack the necessary social skills.

Similarly, children who do not know how to assert or stand up for themselves may find they are targeted victims of bullies. Children need to be able to tell others when their behavior is bothering them. This can be done without starting a fight or hurting someone's feelings. An assertive response is less likely to provoke anger and more likely to get compliance than an aggressive response to abusive or annoying behavior.

Children need to understand how to use their words to assert themselves when faced with inappropriate behavior from another child. A conflict does not have to end with people walking away feeling angry. There is a peaceful way to resolve conflict by using the right words. Allow children time to practice the four components of assertive behavior so they are comfortable with it. Break it down to four simple steps:

1. I state the other person's name
2. I say how I feel

3. I describe the behavior that I don't like
4. I tell them what I want them to do

Start by having the children describe the behavior they don't like and how they feel about it ("I was watching television when you changed the channel. I don't like that."). Once children are able to do that, teach them to make a request for a new behavior. Tell children that just asking someone to stop isn't always successful, but that the other person may be likely to change their behavior if they receive a good suggestion about what to do instead. Here are a few examples to demonstrate:

When another takes your property without asking, you might say: "Jack, I get mad when you take my stuff and don't ask. I want it back."
or when someone calls you a mean name: "Jason, I don't like being called names. It really gets me angry. I want you to stop it."
or when someone "cuts" in front of you on the lunch line: "Ashley, I get angry when you push in front of me. I want you to go back in line."

It's important to notice and point out the difference between being assertive and aggressive. The focus in assertiveness is on yourself (your feelings, what you don't like, and what you want), while the focus in aggressiveness is on the other person (attacking the other person verbally or physically). This is why assertiveness is less provoking to others and more successful at resolving conflicts. A side note is needed here though. This is a strategy to use with someone you know: a friend, classmate, or parent. It is usually not effective or recommended when dealing with a stranger acting like a bully.

PRACTICE, PRACTICE, PRACTICE

We've heard the old adage that "practice makes perfect." In order for children to master these skills they need to practice them over and over. Children love to role-play and this is a great activity to have fun with and at the same time reinforce these skills. Make a game of it. Describe hypothetical situations and have children respond. Here is a sample list to select from. Add more of your own.

1. John keeps calling you "four eyes" because you wear glasses.
2. You are so angry with George, you feel like hitting him. What do you do to cool down?
3. There is one box of crayons, but three of you want to color.
4. Only one last straw in the cafeteria, and you and Ashley want it.
5. By accident you bump into Brian, and he gets upset because he thinks you did it on purpose.
6. You are very angry because James did not select you for his team. Use self-talk to cool off.
7. Jessica knocks over your tower of blocks.
8. There is only one cookie left, and both you and Sarah want it.

Be sure to point out and praise what the child did correctly and suggest ways to further improve his or her response.

21

TEACHING FRIENDSHIP SKILLS

Making and Keeping Friends

"To have a friend, you must be a friend."

—Ralph Waldo Emerson

Teaching children how to make and keep friends is probably one of the most valuable things that parents and teachers can do to prevent bullying. Children who have a strong network of friends feel a sense of belonging, are happy, and feel good about themselves. If others like them, they can like themselves! Keep in mind that bully power gets its strength from isolating its victims. The best prey for bullies are victims who have no friends, no one to talk to, and no one to defend them. The victims are on their own to fend for themselves. They have no friends to offer help and support. They are the perfect targets.

A strong foundation of friendship skills will last an entire lifetime with great benefits to gain at the age of 5, 15, 25, 35, 65, and 95. Humans are social animals. Friends help build our self-esteem and make us feel good about ourselves as well as give us an opportunity to share and enjoy life with others. The development and meaning of friendship changes as children get older. Simply sharing activities and toys defines a close friendship for five- to six-year-olds. They will play with almost anyone. By the time children reach the age of 11 and 12, close friendships are based on common interests. Close friends now are supportive and understand each other. So how do

TEACHING FRIENDSHIP SKILLS

we teach our children those all-important friendship skills? Again, we begin at an early age.

MODEL FRIENDSHIP

Children learn a lot about friendship by watching their parents. They observe closely as parents interact with others. If the parent is a recluse, don't expect their child to be an outgoing, friendly type. However, if parents are friendly and really value friendship, and if their lifestyles reflect this, their children have a head start. They have friendly models to imitate. Remember the apple doesn't fall far from the tree. Inviting friends over routinely for dinner or a social gathering or maybe an afternoon barbecue when the children are present gives them an opportunity to observe, participate, and reflect on what friendship is about.

NURTURE YOUR CHILD'S INTERESTS
IN INTERACTIVE ACTIVITIES

Sean is seven years old and loves to play video games and read. He hasn't spent much time on play dates at others' houses. He's great at entertaining himself in his room. But at school when the others are playing ball, Sean is in the sandbox by himself. In the classroom during rainy day activities, he sits and reads because he doesn't know how to play checkers or the other board games.

At home parents need to nurture children's interests in a variety of things and activities that will attract friendships. Activities like sports, board games, creative pretending, and doll play require two to play and interact, while activities like watching television and playing video games don't require conversation to take place or children to really play together. In school and in the classroom, friendships should be encouraged through cooperative work and play. Children should be given opportunities to work together on school assignments one-on-one and in small groups. On the playground, children should learn and participate in team sports.

Select interactive toys and activities to learn for both inside and outside the house. They should be age appropriate and require at least two to play. The good news is if children enjoy them, they must seek out friends to play them. Choose a game that you, as the parent, will find fun to play with your child, because you will be teaching it. In making your selection, choose something that has simple rules and doesn't take too long to play. To get ideas, just observe children at recess. You'll find that balls and jump ropes are good. Purchase some chalk and teach your child hopscotch. Six and seven year olds are able to play Candyland, checkers, Parcheesi, Chutes and Ladders, and Mr. Wiggley. Just check the recommended ages listed on the game box.

Begin by teaching your child the activity or game. Have fun playing the game with your child to develop an interest and knowledge of the game. There is nothing worse than watching two young children get impatient with each other when they don't know how to play a game. Allowing children to win occasionally when playing with the parent will further encourage participation. When children lose all the time they get quite frustrated and turn off. With an arsenal of interactive activities that children enjoy and know how to play, it's time to set up a play date.

SET UP PLAY DATES

Give children a lot of exposure to other children starting at a young age. Children learn how to get along with their peers and others with practice. The best way to learn to be a friend is through one-on-one play dates. Though organized classes and sports help children meet each other, there isn't usually much of an opportunity to really get to know each other. One to two play dates (for two hours) a week would suffice as a minimum for second graders and older; a shorter period is needed for five- to six-year-olds and younger.

For many parents sometimes the hardest task is to find time to set up and have playmates over to the house. We all lead busy lives, usually with both parents working, making it easy to just "veg out" on the weekends. Children may be great at entertaining themselves. That certainly is a plus and gives parents that precious time for themselves. But be careful not to fall into that trap of letting children engage in so much solo play like video games, reading, and television watching that there is no opportunity to learn how to cultivate friendships. Similarly, be careful not to over schedule or fill up a child's time with so many activities that there is no time to just play and have fun with friends. A child doesn't need dance, soccer, music lessons, gymboree, and girl scouts every week. Prioritize the activities so that children are able to have those one-on-one play dates with other children and learn to establish close relationships.

SUPERVISE YOUNG CHILDREN'S PLAY

Being nearby with an ear open and eyes behind your head can serve children well. Both in the home and in the classroom, watching children play can be very informative for parents and teachers. Young children (ages three to four) or immature children need the adult supervision in the play area and maybe even parent involvement in the play to prevent aggressive behavior. Older children don't necessarily have to be "under your nose." Observation can give a parent valuable feedback about children's friendship skills.

This is also a golden opportunity for parents to coach children on how to be a friend. Watch as the children play. Praise the children often and give them treats for exhibiting friendly behaviors. This will reinforce those skills and cause them to be repeated. Say things like:

I really liked the way you shared that box of crayons.
I liked how you helped John pick up the blocks. Good friends help each other.
Good friends let others go first sometimes.

You were very patient waiting your turn.

That was wonderful that you let Jack play with your favorite truck. You are a good friend.

I liked the way you used your words and told Ashley not to grab the doll from you.

You guys played so well today—not one fight. How about a special treat: cookies.

Similarly, when observing inappropriate behavior, a parent may want to question it or point out a positive replacement behavior. Say things like:

What are the rules of the game? Should we change them?

You are the hostess, and a good friend may want to let his guest go first.

Friends are kind to each other. They don't call each other names.

Ashley is crying. A friend cares and might want to talk and try to cheer her up.

If a friend knocks over another friend's blocks, what should a friend say and do?

READ BOOKS AND TALK ABOUT FRIENDSHIP

Books and stories are a great way for children to learn about friendship (see the appendix for a list of recommended books). Reading and talking about friendship is a great opportunity to teach children what a friend is and how to be a friend. Discuss important friendship concepts with children. Important principles to cover include:

A Friend Is Someone Who

Cares about me
Is kind
Helps when I need help
Shares

Cheers me up when I feel sad
Makes me feel good
Is honest with me

How to Be a Friend

Live by the Golden Rule—treat others the way you want to be treated. Be kind and respectful.

Be honest with your friends, and gentle.

Be supportive in good times and bad. Stick up for them. Give advice.

Accept your friends for who they are.

Be friendly—just because they are your friends. You need to put effort into maintaining that friendship.

Friends make mistakes—apologize if you do and accept an apology if your friend does.

Friendship No-No's

A Friend Doesn't

Tease
Hit you
Exclude you
Insult you with mean words
Act selfishly or disrespectfully
Expect you to be something you're not
Tell you what to do and act bossy

MAKING FRIENDS

A good place to start learning how to make friends is at the park or in a small playgroup (mommy-and-me group) where children frequently see each other but haven't yet played together. As with any skill, children become better and better at it the more they are given an opportunity to employ and use the skill. The more experience children are given being around other children, the more likely it is that they will develop strong friendship skills and be comfortable with their peers.

Teach children that finding friends means they must look for them. Tell them that friends come in all sizes, ages, colors, and shapes. Point out that there are a lot of other kids also looking for friends. Show children how to be assertive and not always wait for others to approach them. Practice or role-play with children how to approach another and strike up a conversation. They need to know that if they are turned down, it's okay. Maybe that child is shy or wants to be alone. Encourage them to approach others. Praise children when they assert themselves and try to be friendly.

THE BASICS

Smile and talk to people. Sometimes this first step is the hardest step, especially if children are a bit shy. A smile on the face is welcoming to others. Tell children not to be afraid to smile and say hi to others they see around frequently. They will realize that the child is just being friendly. The talking part will often follow. Conversing doesn't come naturally to all, but with practice it does get a lot easier. A good start is asking people questions. People like it when others are interested in them. It makes them feel good. Tell them about yourself.

Be a good listener. Remember, a conversation involves speaking and listening between two parties. It should be an equal balance. Don't talk too much; that's rather boring after awhile. Give the other person the "floor" and actively listen. Look the person in the eye and show with a nod that you are hearing them. People like to be listened to. It makes them feel that what they are saying is important to you, that you are interested in them.

Be kind, compliment people. Treating others the way you want to be treated, with respect, will make you many friends. Find something nice about the way other children look or do something, and tell them. Everyone likes to hear positive things about themselves.

Invite people to sit with you at lunch, play on the schoolyard, come to your home, and so forth. Interacting with kids one-on-one allows you to get to know each other.

KEEPING FRIENDS

How do you keep friends? Teach children that the best way to keep friends is by being a friend; it's as easy as that. Probably the biggest difficulty keeping friends is failure to work at the friendship. Tell children they should assert themselves. If they want a person to be their friend, let them know it. This means not waiting for the other person to engage them in talk. Invite them for a get-together or call them up and ask how they are. Being friendly is the key.

Review what qualities people look for in friends and help children to examine and rate themselves as a friend. Whenever these qualities are observed in children's behavior, point them out and compliment children. Here are some examples of what you might say:

> You acted like a good friend by trying to cheer Jason up when he was upset.
>
> That's great that you are helping Ashley with her homework. You are a good friend.
>
> That was nice of you to share your toys (or food) with Ben. That's what friends do.
>
> That was nice that you called Jessica at home when she was absent from school today and probably home sick. You acted like a friend who cares.
>
> That was great when you told Jen not to pick on Samantha. Friends stand up for each other.

In this way you are not only defining what friendship is but also reinforcing positive friendship behaviors.

CLASSROOM-TESTED LESSONS ON FRIENDSHIP

This is a series of three lessons on friendship—what friendship is, and how to make and keep friends—that can be taught to all ages. These may be used in the classroom or at home.

Lesson: What Is a Friend?

Background

Children who have a network of friends socially fit in and feel good about themselves. This sense of belonging and being liked by others increases self-esteem. Moreover, children with friends are less likely to become targets of bullies.

Expected Outcome

Children will learn the essence of friendship—how to act like a friend as well as how to make and keep friends.

Children Learn

A friend is kind, caring, helpful, and sharing. To make friends, we need to be assertive and act friendly—smiling, approaching others, and starting conversations. To keep friends, we must treat them with respect and keep working at our friendships: talking, sharing, helping, and enjoying each other's company. It is friendly to include others who are playing by themselves.

Introduction

Say: *Let's think about a good friend you have now. How would you describe your friend? What qualities do you like most about him or her?*

Write the qualities that the children give you on the board or paper. Keep the list to add additional traits later on. (Note: All qualities/traits should be acceptable. If students give you behaviors—equate them to traits. For example, "A friend gives you part of his lunch when you forget yours"—A friend shares). Conversely, when children give you a trait, request an example of behavior that shows that quality. For example: A friend is someone who cares—He calls me up at home when I am absent from school.

On the blackboard or a piece of paper write:

A Friend Is Someone Who:

Quality	Behavior
Shares	Gives me some of his cookies
Cares	Calls me up when I am sick

Activities

1. Pair each child up with someone he or she does not know too well and have them interview each other. Find out as much as you can and present him or her to the group or class.
2. Have groups of two to four children work together to create a "Friend Ship." On the ship list the four most important qualities they look for in a friend.
3. Children rate themselves as a friend—What are their strongest qualities as a friend? (Older children can write them down; younger children express orally.)

Lesson 2: Making Friends

Background

The act of approaching others to make friends is difficult for many, even adults. A wonderful opportunity exists here to role-play an important social skill and practice being assertive. The more the children practice this, the more comfortable they will be doing it.

Lesson

Start a discussion: *Think about a friend that you made in the past. How did you make this friend?* Let the children discuss the various ways that they made friends. *Suppose you were at the park and saw someone you thought you'd like to meet. What would you do and say? Is it hard sometimes to approach others? Why? If someone doesn't want to be your friend, what then?*

Say: *Today, we're going to practice making new friends.* Ask for a volunteer (Sarah, "S") to role-play with you ("T") pretending to be on a playground. The script might go like this:

T: Hi, I'm Terry, what's your name? (Point out that you are smiling/making eye contact)

S: Jackie. (who is jumping rope)

T: You jump rope really well.

S: Thanks.

T: Can I jump with you?

S: Sure.

T: Whose class are you in?

S: Miss Raven. Whose class are you in?

T: Miss Stern. Is Miss Raven nice? (and so on)

Analyze and evaluate the role-play guided questions:

How did I approach Sarah?
What did you notice about my demeanor? Voice? Face?
What did I do first?
What did I talk about?
Was there anything that I said that was particularly effective?
What other things could I have started talking about?

Review the how-to steps that were taken:

1. Pick a time when someone is not busy with something or someone else. Selecting someone who is alone is a good opportunity.
2. Go up to him or her and introduce yourself. "Hi, my name is _____, what's yours?" Smile, make eye contact, and have a cheerful tone in your voice that is friendly and inviting.

3. Begin a conversation. You might want to decide ahead of time what you want to say, depending on whether this is someone you know, have just seen around, or don't know. You can start off by paying someone a compliment or talking about your favorite TV show or movie you just saw, hobbies, school, etc.
4. Invite the person to play a game, such as basketball or hopscotch, or ask him or her if you can join in what he or she is doing.

Role-Play

Encourage all to participate. Set up a variety of role-plays (for example: a new student comes to the school, or you are at a party). Tell the kids to be creative. The only requirement is to be friendly and get to know the other person. Friendships don't occur after one conversation. They take time.

Activity Assignment

Approach someone you don't know, or who you don't know well, at recess and practice the four steps above.

Lesson 3: Keeping Friends

Discussion

Think about a friend that you have had for a while. How have you stayed friends? What do you do to keep your friends? How do your friendships get stronger? Make a list of the responses from the students. Point out that most of the responses enhance the friendship because you are getting to know each other better by talking together, getting together, sharing, etc. A friendship grows in time. It is something we have to work at.

Activities

1. Write an essay with a partner: "To have a friend, you must be a friend." What does this quote mean when it comes to making and keeping friends?

2. Develop friendships in small groups:

    Grades K–3: a) Pass out four to five M&Ms per student. Each M&M should represent a favorite thing (red = favorite food; orange = favorite TV show; green = favorite color, and so on). b) Hold up an M&M and have the children share the corresponding information with the group. c) Eat the M&M.

    Grades 4–12: a) Assign partners by giving out numbers. b) Put a timer on for two to three minutes as each pair finds out as many interesting things as they can about their partners. c) Share what you found out with the group.

3. Circle of friends can be a routine activity that children participate in, in a class or small group. It is basically a chat group. The object is to get to know each other better. Anyone—parent, teacher, or the children—can propose themes to talk about for each meeting. Talking about new friendships and how they made them might be one theme.

APPENDIX
Recommended Children's Reading List

AGES 2-5

Bootsie Barker Bites by Barbara Bottner (ages 2–5)
I'll Fix Anthony by Judith Viorst (ages 2–5)
No Regard Beauregard and the Golden Rule by James Rice (ages 2–5)
Hazel's Amazing Mother by Rosemary Wells (ages 2–5)
Swimmy by Leo Lionni (ages 2–5)
Why Are You Mean to Me? by Deborah Hautig (ages 2–5)

AGES 3-8

Abby's Wish by Liza St. John (ages 4–8)
The Ant Bully by John Nickle (ages 4–7)
Arthur's April Fool by Marc Brown (ages 4–8)
The Berenstain Bears and the Bully by Stan and Jan Berenstain (ages 4–8)
Berenstain Bears and the "In Crowd" by Stan and Jan Berenstain (ages 4–8)
Best Enemies by Kathleen Leverich (ages 4–8)
Best Enemies Again by Kathleen Leverich (ages 4–8)
Best Enemies Forever by Kathleen Leverich (ages 4–8)
The Big Squeal by J. Scaglione and G. Small (ages 3–8)

Bully for the Beast by Kathleen Stevens (ages 4–8)

Bully Trouble by Joanne Cole (ages 4–8)

Camp Big Paw by Doug Cushman (ages 4–8)

Camp Sink or Swim by Gibbs Davis (ages 4–8)

Crow Boy by Taro Yashima (ages 4–8)

Franklin's Secret Club by Paulette Bourgeois (ages 4–8)

Goggles! by Ezra Jack Keats (ages 4–8)

Happy Birthday Ronald Morgan by Patricia Reilly Giff (ages 4–8)

Hooway for Wodney Wat by Helen Lester (ages 5–8)

How to Lose All Your Friends by Nancy Carlson (ages 4–7)

How to Handle Bullies, Teasers, and Other Meaners by Kate Cohen-Posey (ages 4–7)

Martha Walks the Dog by Susan Meddaugh (ages 4–8)

Joshua T. Bates in Trouble Again by Susan Shreve (ages 4–8)

Nobody Knew What to Do by Becky Ray McCain (ages 4–8)

The New Girl at School by Judy Delton (ages 4–8)

The Recess Queen by Alexis O'Neil (ages 3–7)

No More Bullying by Rosemary Stones (ages 4–8)

Odd Velvet by Mary Whitcomb and Tara King (ages 3–8)

Oliver Button Is a Sissy by Tomie DePaola (ages 4–8)

Our Veronica by Roger Duvoisin (ages 3–7)

Pinky and Rex and the Bully by James Howe (ages 4–8)

Starring First Grade by Miriam Cohen (ages 4–8)

Stay Away From Simon by Carol Carrick (ages 4–8)

Stop Picking on Me by Pat Thomas and Lesley Harber (ages 4–8)

Tyrone, the Double Dirty Rotten Cheater by Hans Wilheim (ages 4–8)

Tyrone the Horrible by Hans Wilheim (ages 4–8)

The Very Bad Bunny by Marilyn Sadler (ages 4–8)

Welcome Comfort by Patricia Polacco (ages 4–8)

AGES 9–14

A Dog on Barkham Street by Mary Stolz (ages 9–12)

Afternoon of the Elves by Janet Lisle (ages 9–12)

Bad Girls by Cynthia Voigt (ages 9–12)

The Bears' House Marilyn Sachs (ages 9–12)

The Best Christmas Pageant Ever by Barbara Robinson (ages 9–12)

The Best School Year Ever by Barbara Robinson (ages 9–12)

Blubber by Judy Blume (ages 9–12)

The Boy Who Lost His Face by Louis Sachar (ages 9–12)

Bridge to Terabithia by Katherine Paterson (ages 9–12)

Bullies Are a Pain in the Brain by Trevor Romain (ages 9–12)

The Bully of Barkham Street by Mary Stolz (ages 9–12)

Cliques, Phonies, and Baloney by Trevor Romain (ages 9–12)

Crash by Jerry Spinelli (ages 10–12)

Ethan Between Us by Anna Myers (ages 12–16)

Flip Flop Girl by Katherine Paterson (ages 12–14)

Freak the Mighty by Rodman Philbrick (ages 9–12)

Fourth Grade Rats by Jerry Spinelli (ages 9–12)

Great Gilly Hopkins by Katherine Paterson (ages 9–12)

Harriet the Spy by Louise Fitzhugh (ages 9–12)

The Hundred Dresses by Eleanor Estes (ages 9–12)

Karen's Bully by Ann Martin (ages 9–12)

King of the Playground by Phyllis Reynolds Naylor (ages 9–12)

Maniac Mcgee by Jerry Spinelli (ages 9–12)

The Middle of the Sandwich by Tim Kennemore (ages 9–12)

Nekomah Creek by Linda Crews (ages 9–12)

Present Takers by Aidan Chambers (ages 9–12)

Randall's Wall by Carol Fenner (ages 9–12)

The Secret of Gumbo Grove by Eleanora Tate (ages 9–12)

A Spoonful of Jam by Michelle Magorian (ages 12–14)

Stick Up for Yourself by Gershen Kaufman (ages 9–12)

Shoebag by Mary James (ages 9–12)

Stepping on the Cracks by Mary Downing Hahn (ages 9–12)

The Tulip Touch by Anne Fine (ages 11–14)

Valentine Rosy by Sheila Greenwald (ages 9–12)

Veronica Ganz by Marilyn Sachs (ages 9–12)

AGES 14 AND UP

Daphne's Book by Mary Downing (ages 14–17)
Dear Mr. Henshaw by Beverly Cleary (ages 14–17)
The Diddakoi by Rumer Golden (ages 14–17)
The Eighteenth Emergency by Betsy Byars (ages 14–17)

REFERENCES

Associated Press. (2003, September 4). Report: Bullies at Risk of Becoming Criminals. Retrieved June 8, 2006, from www.cnn.com/2003/EDUCATION/09/04/sprj.sch.bullying.prevention.ap.

Center for the Prevention of School Violence (2001). Parents Not Overly Concerned About School Environments for Their Children. Gallup News Service.

Early Home Environment and Television Watching Influence Bully Behavior. (2005, April 21). *Journal of the American Medical Association*. Retrieved June 8, 2006, from www.sciencedaily.com/releases/2005/04/050420091955.htm.

Ericson, Nels. (2001, June). Addressing the Problem of Juvenile Bullying. *OJJDP Factsheet* 27.

Fight Crime: Invest in Kids. (2003). Bully Prevention Is Crime Prevention. Retrieved June 8, 2006, from www.fightcrime.org.

I-safeAmerica, Inc. (2005, May). Beware of the Cyberbully. Retrieved November 2005, from www.isafe.org.

I-safeAmerica, Inc. Cyberbully: Statistics and Tips. Retrieved November 2005, from www.isafe.org.

Josephson Institute of Ethics. (2001, April 2). 2000 Report Card: Report #1: The Ethics of American Youth: Violence and Substance Abuse: Data and Commentary. Retrieved June 8, 2006, from www.josephsoninstitute.org/Survey2000/violence2000-commentary.htm.

Kaiser Family Foundation and Nickelodeon. (2001). Talking With Kids About Tough Issues: A National Survey of Parents and Kids. Retrieved June 9, 2006, from www.talkingwithkids.org/nickelodeon/pr-3-8-01.htm.

Limber, S. P., & Small, M. A. (2003). State Laws and Policies to Address Bullying in Schools. *School Psychology Review* 32(3): 445–455.

McGee, M. K. (2005, May 25). School-Yard Bullies Add Internet to Arsenal of Pain. *Information Week*. Retrieved June 9, 2006, from www.information week.com/showArticle.jhtml;jsessionid=IWS03LBFEIVTAQSNDBOCKIC CJUMEKJVN?articleID=163700746&queryText=school+yard+bullies.

Nansel, T. R., Overpeck, M., Pilla, R. S., Ruan,W. J., Simons-Morton, B., & Scheidt, P. (2001). Bullying Behaviors Among U.S. Youth: Prevalence and Association With Psychosocial Adjustment. *Journal of the American Medical Association* 285: 2094–2100.

National Institute of Child Health and Human Development (NICHD). (2001). Bullying Widespread in U.S. Schools. Retrieved June 9, 2006, from http://parentingteens.about.com/cs/bullying/a/bullying.htm.

Nishina, A., & Juvonen, J. (2005, March). Daily Reports of Witnessing and Experiencing Peer Harassment in Middle School. *Child Development* 76(2): 435–450.

Olweus, D., & Limber, S. (1999). NICHD on the U.S. Contribution to the World Health Behavior in School-Age Children Survey. Retrieved December 2005, from www.safeyouth.org.

Stories About Bullying. Retrieved December 2005, from www.bullybeware .com/index.html (n.d.).

University of California, Los Angeles. (2005, April 11). Bullying Among Sixth Graders a Daily Occurrence, UCLA Study Finds. Retrieved June 8, 2006, from http://www.sciencedaily.com/releases/2005/04/050411100940 .htm.

Walsh, J., The National Center for Missing and Exploited Children (NCMEC), and Cox Communications. (2005, May 25). New Study Reveals Parents Need Better Cybersmarts. Retrieved June 9, 2006, from http://phx .corporate-ir.net/phoenix.zhtml?c=76341&p=irol-newsArticle&t=Regular &id=713625&.

ABOUT THE AUTHORS

Dr. Joanne Scaglione has been a principal, counselor, and teacher in grades K–12 for 30 years. She has written and lectured extensively on the issue of raising happy and successful children in the twenty-first century on television, the internet, and at workshops for parents and educators. As a leader and expert on the topic of bullying, Dr. Scaglione has designed and implemented successful school programs aimed at preventing and stopping it. She is coauthor of two children's books: *The Big Squeal: A Wild, True, and Twisted Tail* (2005) and *Life's Little Lessons: An Inch-by-Inch Tale of Success* (2006).

Arrica Rose Scaglione makes her debut as an author in *Bully-Proofing Children*, a collaboration between mother and daughter, as she brings a fresh and creative approach to the issue of bullying based on her firsthand experiences during her school years. Arrica Rose, a Los Angeles-based singer/songwriter, completed her 2006 national tour, celebrating the release of her highly-acclaimed album, *People Like Us* (pOprOck Records, July 2006). Whether performing acoustic with just her guitar or electric with her band, The Dot Dot Dots, she has been garnering a wealth of glowing reviews and accolades. She is also the cocreator of the award-winning *Dexter and Lucy* children's music series and dance video.